PHILOSOPHY
AND
FICTION

Other AUP titles

THE MEANING OF FREEDOM
Philip Drew

COMMON DENOMINATORS IN ART AND SCIENCE
edited by Martin Pollock FRS

Scots Philosophical Monographs

THINGS THAT HAPPEN
J E Tiles

FREGE'S CONCEPTION OF NUMBERS AS OBJECTS
Crispin Wright

APPROPRIATING HEGEL
Crawford Elder

HISTORICAL EXPLANATION RECONSIDERED
Gordon Graham

PHILOSOPHY AND FICTION

ESSAYS IN LITERARY AESTHETICS

edited by
PETER LAMARQUE

ABERDEEN UNIVERSITY PRESS

First published 1983
Aberdeen University Press
A member of the Pergamon Group

© Aberdeen University Press 1983

British Library Cataloguing in Publication Data

Philosophy and fiction
1. Literature—Aesthetics
I. Lamarque, Peter
801'.93   PN45

ISBN 0-08-030353-6

PRINTED IN GREAT BRITAIN
THE UNIVERSITY PRESS
ABERDEEN

CONTENTS

PREFACE

The essays in this collection originated as contributions to a Scots Philosophical Club conference on Philosophy and Literature at Stirling University in September 1981. Several of the essays have been extensively revised.

On behalf of the Club, I would like to thank all who took part in the conference, either as speakers or visitors, making it a lively and instructive forum of discussion. I would also like to thank Linda Greig for her help with the typing both during the organisation of the conference and in preparation for this volume.

December 1982   PETER LAMARQUE

CONTRIBUTORS

R W BEARDSMORE—lecturer in philosophy at the University College of North Wales, Bangor. Author of *Moral Reasoning* (1969) and *Art and Morality* (1971).

PETER LAMARQUE—lecturer in philosophy at the University of Stirling.

COLIN LYAS—senior lecturer in philosophy at the University of Lancaster. Editor of *Philosophy and Linguistics* (1971).

STEIN HAUGOM OLSEN—senior lecturer in English literature at the University of Oslo. Author of *The Structure of Literary Understanding* (1978).

FLINT SCHIER—lecturer in philosophy at the University of Glasgow.

I

INTRODUCTION

Peter Lamarque

These are philosophical essays on a range of topics in the theory of literature. As a collection they owe allegiance to no particular 'school' of criticism or critical theory and even within philosophy they draw on resources from different areas of the subject, including philosophical psychology (on tragedy and emotions), philosophical logic (on fiction) and moral philosophy (on censorship). There is no *philosophical* theory of literature as such in the sense in which we might speak of a psychoanalytic or structuralist or Marxist theory. The philosophical approach reflects a belief that there are fundamental questions about literature and criticism which arise *prior* to the formulation of systematic theories.

The essays are polemical. They directly engage issues of controversy and do not merely reflect on them or survey their history. Each essay develops and defends a specific, sometimes provocative, point of view on its chosen topic. Although ostensibly the topics are varied, there are many overlapping themes and strands of thought. In this Introduction I will identify and characterise some of those and also sketch in some of the background against which the debates are conducted.

I THE NATURE OF LITERARY AESTHETICS

First of all, a word about literary aesthetics, the enquiry to which the essays contribute. Literary aesthetics is that branch of the theory of literature which is (a) distinctively philosophical and which (b) focuses attention on those aspects of literary works in virtue of which they are works of art. The subject matter of literary aesthetics is defined by the specific application to literature of the questions raised in aesthetics about works of art in general. Aesthetics, as a philosophical enquiry, is concerned with analysing the very concept of art, what art *is*, the special attention it commands in human lives, the judgments and evaluations that relate to it, the links between art and morality and truth, as well as such elusive notions as beauty and taste.

Applied to literature these concerns take on a distinctive character. For what sets literature apart from the other arts and introduces a different order of complexity is its essentially *linguistic* nature. A work of literature is

1

not only a work of art, it is also an expression in a language; it has both an aesthetic and a linguistic dimension. A central issue in literary aesthetics is the relation between these two dimensions. As Stein Haugom Olsen has put it:

> ... any intelligible discussion of the literary work as a distinct class of artwork presupposes a systematic connection of some kind between the linguistic and aesthetic features of a work. However, one of the cruxes of literary theory has been the nature of the aesthetic properties and the connection between the text and these properties.[1] (*The Structure of Literary Understanding* (1978)).

In his essay here, Olsen develops further his own theory of the aesthetic properties of literary works and their connection with linguistic properties. I will turn to that in a moment.

We might characterise two important, closely related, aims in literary aesthetics, reflecting philosophical concerns about art in general:

> (1) To identify those features of literary works in virtue of which they are literary works, that is, works of art, thereby establishing a basis for the distinction between the literary and the non-literary;
> (2) To identify those responses to literary works, be they 'critical', emotive or moral, which are integral to a treatment of the works as literature.

All of the essays that follow contribute to facets of these general aims. In the next two sections I will look at some of the debates involved under these two headings.

II THE CONCEPT OF LITERATURE

It is natural to seek the defining characteristics of works of literature in their linguistic dimension. 'Literature,' said Valéry, 'is, and can be nothing other than, a kind of extension and application of certain properties of language.'[2] The suggestion might seem uncontroversial given general agreement about what marks literature off from other art forms. But difficulties soon arise when we try to isolate the requisite properties. For one thing, the idea of a 'property of language' is itself not entirely clear. We might distinguish those properties which are *intrinsic* to language, properties of syntax or semantics, and those which are *extrinsic*, relating to its use, in this case its special function or purpose in literature. Capturing something like this distinction, H G Widdowson speaks of treatments of literature as *text*, concentrating on 'how a piece of literature exemplifies the language system', and treatments of literature as *discourse*, concentrating on 'how pieces of literary writing function as a form of communication'.[3] There are no shortages of proposed definitions of literature that highlight these different approaches.

Characteristic *textual* peculiarities of literary works are not hard to find and literary or poetic 'devices' have been well catalogued and analysed: syntactical 'deviance', predominance of metaphor, compactness, ambiguity,

---

[1] Notes appear at the end of each chapter.

'tension', 'patterns of resolutions and balances and harmonizations', paradox, and so on.[4] An emphasis on textual properties has characterised much formalist theory within the traditions both of American New Criticism and of structuralism, emanating from the Russian and Czech formalist schools. In the aesthetics of New Criticism, for example, an influential theory, known as the 'semantic definition' of literature, was advanced by Monroe Beardsley. Beardsley proposed that literary works could be defined by a particular semantic property of language, the possession by a text of a high degree of 'implicit meaning' or 'connotation'.[5] The idea that literary language is distinctive in having multiple 'layers' of meaning is a familiar notion, encouraged by the practical methods of the New Criticism. But no such intrinsic textual property alone seems adequate to explain the 'literariness' of *all* literary works. It certainly cannot provide necessary and sufficient conditions of 'literariness'; there are just too many exceptions. The focus for theories emphasising textual peculiarities inevitably falls on poetry, often one kind of poetry at that, as a literary paradigm. But, as Malcolm Bradbury has written:

> If you regard novels as 'typical' forms of literature, it becomes somewhat difficult to assume that what distinguishes literary language—what makes literature literature—is those attributes of paradox and tension, those compactnesses of self-sufficient language, that you find crucial in lyric poetry[6] (*Possibilities* (1973)).

Both Olsen and Colin Lyas have produced powerful arguments, in earlier work, against Beardsley's semantic definition and correspondingly against any theory which seeks to define literature in terms of intrinsic linguistic properties of a text.[7] Both point out that such definitions will be fundamentally inadequate in that they fail to explain the *value* we attach to literature. 'Implicit meaning', ambiguity or paradox have no value in themselves and at best can only be a *means* by which other qualities are obtained which we do value; after all, in non-literary discourse, ambiguity and paradox can be a nuisance, a disvalue, even a form of deceit. Lyas writes:

> If someone cites *any* quality and argues that this quality is a defining condition of literature, then that quality must be a quality that will lead to a favourable evaluation of any work exemplifying the quality in question. It will, that is, be impossible to define literature unless we cite features the possession of which makes a piece of writing valuable in a certain way[8] ('The Semantic Definition of Literature' (1969)).

Textual properties in themselves have no literary or aesthetic significance; they only acquire such significance, and thus value, when they are assigned or fulfil some function within a work. We might expect to gain a clearer idea of 'literariness' if we could identify such a function or functions. This suggests that looking at literature as *discourse*, as a use of language with specific purposes, is a more promising approach in the search for a definition of literature.

Again there have been many proposals for explaining the purposes distinctive of literary language. Two suggestions have had particular prominence, though again mainly from theorists of a formalist persuasion: the idea that the function of literary language is *to draw attention to itself*, and the idea of the *fictionality* of literary language. The two ideas are related via a notion of the special *referential* peculiarities of literature.

The first idea emphasises the self-reflexive nature of literary writing, nicely encapsulated in Roland Barthes' essay title 'To Write: an Intransitive Verb'. Roman Jakobson has developed the idea of 'the palpability of signs' in literary language:

> The distinctive feature of poetry lies in the fact that a word is perceived as a word and not merely a proxy for the denoted object or an outburst of an emotion, that words and their arrangement, their meaning, their outward and inward form acquire weight and value of their own[9] (*cit.* Victor Erlich, *Russian Formalism: History-Doctrine* (1965)).

A related notion is that of 'foregrounding', defined by the Czech theorist Jan Mukarovsky as 'the aesthetically intentional distortion of linguistic components'.[10]

> Any item in discourse that attracts attention to itself for what it *is*, rather than acting merely as a vehicle for information, is foregrounded[11] (David Lodge, *The Modes of Modern Writing* (1977)).

According to this view, literary language draws attention to itself as an aesthetic object. Its purpose is conceived as radically different from that of ordinary discourse, at least of the kind that aims to convey thoughts about a world beyond itself. Another associated notion is that of language 'at play', highlighting the 'pleasures' (or *jouissance*) of the written word. A common theme here is the denial of a standard *referential* function for literary discourse.[12] Although the denial does not itself entail that literary works are *self-referential*, this consequence is sometimes drawn:

> Every work, every novel, tells through its fabric of events the story of its own creation, its own history ... the meaning of a work lies in its telling itself, its speaking of its own existence[13] (Tzvetan Todorov, *cit.* T Hawkes, *Structuralism and Semiotics* (1977)).

The second idea, that of the fictionality of literary discourse, has been directly linked with the idea of foregrounding:

> ... literary discourse is either self-evidently fictional or may be read as such, and ... what compels or permits such reading is the structural organization of its component parts, its systematic foregrounding (Lodge, *op. cit.* pp. 6–7).

The suggestion is not that literary works must always be works of fiction— after all, we classify as literature such works as Boswell's *Life of Johnson*, Gibbon's *Decline and Fall* or Hume's *Dialogues Concerning Natural Religion*— only that to read them *as literature* is to read them *as fiction*, in the sense of setting aside referential concerns or concerns with truth or falsity.[14] As Lodge writes: 'Boswell's Johnson then becomes something like a fictional character and his *Life* is read as if it were a kind of novel.'[15] Lodge insists, though, on a class of 'axiomatically literary' works which directly exploit foregrounding for fictional ends; the works mentioned would not belong in this class. Several analytical philosophers have pursued the idea that literary discourse is paradigmatically fictional. The view is sometimes expressed in terms of 'illocutionary acts': these are speech acts such as asserting, questioning, commanding, etc., performed in the uttering of sentences.

> A literary work is a discourse whose sentences lack the illocutionary forces that would normally attach to them. Its illocutionary force is *mimetic* . . . a literary work *purportedly imitates* (or reports) a series of speech acts, which in fact have no other existence[16] (Richard Ohmann, 'Speech Acts and the Definition of Literature' (1971)).

Literary works on this view, at least those whose purpose is primarily literary rather than, say, historical or philosophical, are identified as pretended illocutionary acts. The function of literary language *per se* is not that of performing illocutionary acts, as in non-literary discourse, but of mimicking performances of such acts. So also Beardsley, who came to supplement his semantic definition with a theory of fictionality:[17]

> . . . the writing of a poem, as such, is not an illocutionary act; it is the creation of a fictional character performing a fictional illocutionary act[18] (*The Possibility of Criticism* (1970); also cited by Lyas below, p. 21).

We are now at a point where three of the essays in this collection directly engage the debate about the concept of literature.

(1) Colin Lyas in his essay produces a vigorous and telling critique of the conception of literary works as autonomous aesthetic objects and in particular of the idea that the function of literary language is essentially and exclusively that of pretence. He addresses himself to the view, derived from Beardsley, that

> . . . what makes a literary work a literary work of art . . . has to do with its being a clearly signalled kind of pretence, an act of imaginative creation, an invention or play of the mind that is not to be trammelled with considerations about what the author really thought or felt (Lyas, below, p. 21).

Lyas objects to this pretence theory because in his view it unjustifiably distances the author from the attitudes and beliefs that a work expresses. For example, he emphasises the logical limits on 'what it is possible for a pretender to pretend and what it makes sense for an audience to assume is being pretended'. A writer, he argues, could not successfully *pretend* to show perceptiveness, sensitivity or emotional maturity in a work, which are meritorious qualities, without in fact *possessing* those qualities himself at least on that occasion; the qualities must be *his*, not only his work's. He goes on to press for a distinction between the imaginative *world* of a literary fiction, which is a pretence, and some 'valuational response' to that world in the work which, he argues, need not be a pretence and is often a genuine expression. Although one function of literary language is to create fictional worlds another is to express real attitudes towards those worlds. He rejects the idea that these attitudes must always be attributed to a further fictional invention, an 'implied author' or 'controlling intelligence', distinct from the real author.[19]

Lyas identifies a 'master thought' underlying his argument: that 'a work of art . . . records for us a complex response of a real person to a situation, real or imagined' (below, p. 36). This master thought indicates a radical opposition in Lyas to a view of literature common to both New Criticism and structuralism which systematically distances literary discourse from the imaginative roots of its production. Consider a typical statement of the position he opposes:

> There is no question of Balzac being thought of as 'expressing himself' in *Sarrasine* because that would be Idealism. . . . For [Barthes] a writer's 'self' is a convention of the text of which he is the author, a 'creature of paper' or else an 'effect of language'. The writer . . . is not a substantive presence to be located, as in the past, 'behind' the text. . . . Much of his reality has had to be sacrificed because language is an objective, collective system which we can only use, never expropriate. The real 'I' is thus debarred from ever putting in an appearance[20] (John Sturrock, *Structuralism and Since* (1979)).

Lyas' rejection of this formalist tendency in literary theory has important consequences, as we shall see, for his view of critical practice.

(2) My own essay confronts fictionality directly, in particular the logical peculiarities of 'the language of fiction' and the nature of fictional characters. Again, conclusions are drawn which are at odds with the view that literary fictions are totally *cut off* from the real world. I readily accept that works of fiction, by their very nature, are offered with different *referential* intentions from those of historical or non-fictional writing; the writer is not attempting to recount facts so much as to construct and present imaginative worlds with fictional people and events. But a theory of fiction must be able to account for the *similarities* between these imaginative worlds and the real world, as well as their differences. A writer is not writing *in vacuo*; he draws on reality, and must do so, for the substance of his fictions. In turn the fictional works reflect a reality beyond themselves and no doubt capture our interest precisely on that account. The idea of *mimesis* occupies an enduring place in literary theory though its logic is not always clearly understood. The enquiry I pursue is that of explaining what relations *can* obtain between the imaginative constructs of fiction and things in the real world.

One of my theoretical conclusions is that fictional characters, from the point of view of the real world, can be thought of as *abstract* entities constituted out of properties which are identified through the descriptions of a fictional narrative.[21] A novel-reader can 'recognise reality' in fictions by recognising properties or combinations of properties which he finds exemplified in people or objects of his acquaintance. Although fictions might not be about actual people or things in the world there is no reason to conclude either that they are about *nothing at all* or that they are about *themselves*. Fictional narratives make sense to us and encourage us to picture their imaginative worlds because they employ general terms with the same meaning as in descriptions of the real world; through these general terms they identify attributes and attitudes, thoughts and predicaments which we can quite properly say that the fictions are *about*. On this account, we can see what it might mean to read literature *as fiction*. This would at least partly entail concentrating on the *properties* identified in the work, rather than on the actual *particulars.* Our concern for Boswell's Johnson as a fictional character is a concern with the attitudes and anecdotes ascribed to him *in themselves* and not with their correspondence to facts in the real world.

Sometimes discussions of 'the language of fiction' become confused through failing to distinguish what a *writer* is doing in presenting a fictional character and what a *reader* might be doing in a subsequent description of that character. Readers, or critics, talking about fictional characters can surely make true or false claims about them but it seems wrong to say that a writer in telling a story is himself saying anything true or false.[22] This distinction is emphasised in my essay. In speaking of a writer's use of descriptions, I discuss the 'pretence' view of fictional narrative, as raised by Lyas. Through consideration of a passage from *Tom Jones*, I argue that although there is pretence of reference and assertion, nevertheless, there are genuine illocutionary acts which are not pretended and which can be attributed directly to the author. Here I agree with Lyas that an author need not completely disappear as a 'controlling intelligence' behind the language of fiction.

(3) Olsen in his essay gives extended consideration to the relation between the textual features of a literary work and its aesthetic features.[23] It is the aesthetic features, he argues, that 'constitute the text a literary work' but these aesthetic features cannot be reduced to textual features.

> A textual feature is a feature of style, content or structure. These are features possessed by all texts. All texts have phonological, syntactic, semantic and a minimum of rhetorical features. All texts have a content which can be described in various ways; and all texts structure their content and their formal features in some way. Textual features can be identified by everybody who masters the language in which the text is written (Olsen, below, p. 43).

But mastery of the language is not sufficient to understand or appreciate a piece of discourse *as literature*. Literary appreciation, according to Olsen, calls for judgments of a distinctive kind, aesthetic judgments, which presuppose concepts and conventions embodied in a 'practice' or 'institution'. As he has written elsewhere:

> Without certain practices and conventions over and above the conventions and practices of language, the reader would get nowhere by just looking at a text. Only people in a community which has practices and rules for dealing with literary works can discover anything specifically literary in a text (*The Structure of Literary Understanding*, p. 16).

Olsen is committed to more than an epistemological claim about what readers can and cannot discover. There is a fundamental logical point as well. For according to Olsen, the practice *creates the possibility* of a reader's responding to a text *as a literary work*; without the concepts and conventions of the institution *there would be no literary works*.

Olsen's view here offers a radical re-orientation of the distinction between literary and non-literary discourse. He sees the distinction as residing not in objective properties of language, either intrinsic or functional, but in complex attitudes as defined by the institution.

The identification of something as a literary work is not a matter merely of noting textual and structural facts, but rather a matter of taking up a certain attitude to a text, an attitude involving the reader's commitment to certain assumptions about how he is to deal with it. . . . It is thus, to a certain extent, at the reader's discretion whether he will see a text as a literary work or not. To a certain extent only, because, though he may in theory view any text as a literary work, most texts prove resistant to treatment in literary terms. When, at the same time, these texts are clearly intended to fulfil some other purpose, it will be absurd to insist on treating them as literary works (*The Structure of Literary Understanding*, p. 49).

For Olsen, a literary work is a work that invites and rewards a certain kind of attention. What constitutes a literary work are not objectively given textual features but aesthetic features. These aesthetic features can be identified only within an interpretative judgment 'which assigns to (a) textual feature its significance' according to the conventions of the institution. In his essay here, Olsen gives a clear illustration of what might count as an aesthetic feature. At the climax of Aeschylus' *Agamemnon*, Agamemnon is persuaded by Clytemnestra to step on a carpet; a description is given of the colour of this carpet. The description in itself is a textual feature but, according to Olsen, it becomes an aesthetic feature if the colour is assigned some aesthetic significance under an interpretation; the interpretation, for example, might attribute to the colour a symbolic value connecting it to other elements in the play. An aesthetic judgment is required to identify the colour of the carpet as having symbolic significance. But only under this *redescription* does the colour, linked now into a pattern or network of meaning, become an aesthetic feature in the work. Redescription of this kind is part of what is entailed by a treatment of the text in literary terms.

Aesthetic features, on Olsen's view, are not objective *data* (they are properties of 'emergent' not natural objects[24]); nor can they be read off mechanically in the way that, e.g. syntactic features of a sentence might be identified through formal procedures. Olsen is strongly opposed to any such 'scientific' view of literary criticism.[25] As readers we have access to aesthetic features only through appreciation; what is required is an 'imaginative reconstruction'.[26] In the next section, comparisons will be drawn between Olsen's account of appreciation as a distinctive response to literature and other accounts of literary response.

III   RESPONSES TO LITERARY WORKS

I have discussed debates about the concept of literature and the distinction between literary and non-literary discourse. On Olsen's institutional account of literature the question of *what literature is* is logically connected to our second question of *what responses are appropriate to literature*. Let us address that second question directly.

What is a distinctively *literary* reading of a text? What is it to read a text *as literature*? No question in literary theory is so fraught with controversy. For here we are involved in fundamental issues about the correct procedures of critical practice. Olsen, in previously published work, has offered a detailed and systematic account of the procedures that he sees as constitutive of the institution of literature: in particular the constraints on interpretation and evaluation. His aim has not been to *impose* methods on critics but simply to *describe* basic presuppositions of a well-established practice. Other theorists have attempted a similar enquiry.[27] Jonathan Culler in *Structuralist Poetics* has even drawn an analogy between discovering the underlying rules of critical method and describing the grammar of a language. He uses the term 'literary competence', echoing Chomsky's notion of linguistic competence, to reflect the parallel. He sees the task of poetics as comparable to that of linguistics:

> The question is not what actual readers happen to do but what an ideal reader must know implicitly in order to read and interpret works in ways which we consider acceptable, in accordance with the institution of literature[28] (*Structuralist Poetics* (1975)).

It might seem optimistic of Olsen and Culler to suppose that there is a sufficiently well-defined institution of literature, with conventions sufficiently determinate, to make such an enquiry possible. The matter is indeed debatable. Yet there do seem to be clearly recognisable limits to what is acceptable in critical reasoning; not any response counts as *understanding* a literary work and both interpretative and evaluative judgments invite rational support. One of the tasks of literary aesthetics is to map these limits and to identify the canons of critical judgment.

Olsen's essay here is an important contribution to this exercise. He relates the elusive notion of appreciation to interpretation and evaluation, though stresses the distinctness of each. Olsen insists on the conventional, and indeed intellectual, nature of literary appreciation; it is not a 'natural' response, though it might seem so to a trained reader, and it is not possible without a shared background of concepts and conventions. Appreciation is an experience articulated through an interpretative description. It is a matter of degree, subject to levels of discrimination; a 'measure of the adequacy of discrimination is that it maximises the number of textual features assigned aesthetic significance'. Along the way, Olsen offers some provocative criticisms of psychoanalytic interpretation as part of a general argument that the experience we value in our response to literature is *an end in itself*.

It is interesting to compare Olsen's account of what it is to appreciate literature as literature with Flint Schier's account in his essay of our responses to tragedy, particularly as Olsen uses an example from Greek tragedy to illustrate his discussion. Schier is concerned to explain certain anomalies about our responses to tragedy. Why is it that we *value* tragedies and voluntarily seek them out in the theatre in the clear knowledge that they can cause us distress and pain? Moreover, how are we to explain these emotions? Can we be distressed at a spectacle without the belief that actual suffering is taking place? Schier examines different explanations for our interest in tragedy and our responses to it, using as his starting point the discussion in Hume's essay 'Of Tragedy'.

Schier's own proposal associates the value we attach to tragedy (a) with the distinctive experience we acquire from it, and (b) with a particular type of understanding that it demands. The experience of tragedy in an aesthetic representation must be distinguished from the experience of actual suffering in the real world:

> ... tragedy makes possible for us something which is not possible outside of imaginative experience: the vivid, powerful realization of what it is like to suffer. ... This knowledge is apparently of a very peculiar kind—it is an end in itself (Schier, below, p. 85)

The experience 'is valued, and valued intrinsically, precisely insofar as it arouses certain emotions (pity and empathetic terror)'. But when we react to tragic characters in fiction

> our reaction is necessarily governed by *how* they are represented, and the kind of emotion that it is appropriate to feel is determined by the quality of the representation (Schier, below, p. 85).

He goes on to argue that a true understanding of tragedy, that is, a sympathetic understanding or *Verstehen*, for one who is within the 'community of sentiment', *requires* rather than suppresses an emotional reaction. 'Certain emotional reactions ... may be said to be *criterial* for this kind of understanding' (p. 89). In turn these reactions are a tribute to the work as a work of art.

Schier's argument may give comfort to those who object to Olsen's intellectualist view of literary appreciation which seems to exclude emotional response. There are indeed differences here between the two theorists and Olsen has elsewhere criticised 'the doctrine of sympathy' in literary understanding.[29] But perhaps Schier and Olsen are not so far apart. For one thing, Schier compares our emotional reactions to tragedy with Kantian judgments of taste; he sees them constrained by considerations of appropriateness and essentially connected to the aesthetic qualities of a work. Also, Olsen would not of course deny the propriety of emotional response to literature; he would claim only that emotions are, strictly speaking, *external* to the constitutive procedures of literary criticism.[30]

Schier's essay relates also to that of Lyas. Schier writes:

> One of the pleasures ... of seeing a tragedy, however bleak, stems from our interaction with the controlling intelligence of the artist. The characters to whom we react or fail to respond are the product of that intelligence and our reactions constitute a kind of judgment of his work—of him insofar as he manifests himself in his work. Thus, we are reacting to characters as vividly seen and realized by a controlling intelligence and we respond to the work as an expression of that achieved vision (Schier, below, p. 85).

Lyas would agree that our response to a literary work is at least partly a response to its author. His position has clear consequences for the appropriate procedures of critical study and of course it engages a perennial debate in literary theory about the place to be accorded the author in discussions of literary works. The relevance of any appeal in literary criticism to an author's attitudes and intentions remains a matter of heated controversy even thirty-five years after the publication of 'The Intentional Fallacy'.[31] Each generation of theorists finds arguments to support the contrary positions.

> ... where a text is attributed to a single, named individual, Derrida's argument is that the text has in fact been set free from the individual who produced it. ... An author can have no special authority over what he has written and then published, because he has committed it both to strangers and to the future. The meanings it will henceforth yield need not coincide with those he believed he had invested in it: they will depend on who reads it and in what circumstances (Sturrock, *Structuralism and Since*, p. 14).

Or, in opposition:

> There is a logical connection between statements about the meaning of a literary work and statements about the author's intentions such that a statement about the meaning of a work *is* a statement about the author's intentions[32] (P D Juhl, *Interpretation, An Essay in the Philosophy of Literary Criticism* (1980)).

In an earlier paper 'Personal Qualities and the Intentional Fallacy' (1973), Lyas introduced a new dimension into this somewhat tired debate by identifying and analysing a range of descriptions commonly employed by critics as terms of merit or demerit applied to works of art: responsible, mature, intelligent, sensitive, shallow, vulgar, self-indulgent, etc. He classified these as 'personal qualities' and went on to argue

> that the presence of these qualities in a work reflect the personality of an artist. Hence, if they are relevant things for critics to mention in talking of works, they become critical remarks about the work's creator.[33]

Lyas showed that it is in fact common practice among critics to use such terms and, by exploring the implications of such use, sought to establish the conclusion that there is 'no radical separation of personal and poetic studies'.

His present essay should be seen as a continuation and extension of this argument. Here he seeks to show that it is impossible to draw a sharp distinction between the *sincerity of a work* and the *sincerity of its creator*. Again, if his argument is correct it amounts to a serious erosion of the austere constraints on critical practice imposed by the autonomy view of literature. Another underlying 'master thought' in Lyas' essay is that 'in the last resort the answer to the question 'What is relevant in the criticism of art?' is determined by what human beings find interesting and important in art' (pp. 35–6). For Lyas the attitudes of authors to their subject matter can never be eliminated from literary critical concern: there are logical reasons for this but also reasons based on natural interests we have in works of literature.

IV   LITERATURE AND MORALITY

Finally, Richard Beardsmore in his essay on censorship is also concerned with responses to literary works, in this case with moral judgments. His essay stands apart from the others in that it does not directly discuss properties of literary works or procedures of criticism. Nevertheless, it engages a controversy in the theory of literature with of course far-reaching ramifications elsewhere.

There is an aestheticist view of literature and art, still in evidence today, which sees art itself as a kind of self-contained moral category. For example:

> Once we have judged a thing a work of art, we have judged it ethically of the first importance and put it beyond the reach of the moralist. . . . To pronounce anything a work of art . . . is to credit an object with being so direct and powerful a means to good that we need not trouble ourselves about any other of its consequences[34] (Clive Bell, *Art* (1914)).

Philosophers have been exercised with the moral status of art, and the issue of censorship, as far back as Plato's celebrated attack on the poets in *The Republic*. More recently, the philosophical debate about censorship has tended to be conducted with its terms of reference drawn from the *law* of censorship, in particular, in Britain, with the Obscene Publications Acts. Philosophical concerns here have centred on, for example, the relation of law and morality, the scope of 'freedom of expression' as an ethical presumption, the so-called 'harm condition', definitions of key terms in the law like 'obscene' and 'offensive' and the status of the 'public good defence' relating to artistic merit. A good focus of these concerns can be found in the detailed discussion in the *Report of the Committee on Obscenity and Film Censorship* under the chairmanship of the philosopher Bernard Williams, presented to Parliament in 1979.

One of the premises of the Report is the acceptance of the 'harm condition', that is, the view that 'no conduct should be suppressed by law unless it can be shown to harm someone'.[35] This principle was forcefully and influentially advocated by John Stuart Mill in *On Liberty* (1859). And, as Beardsmore notes, 'much of the discussion of the issues of censorship has been conducted in Mill's terms'. Mill offered an eloquent case against censorship on the grounds that freedom of expression is a fundamental form of freedom. He argued that it was up to each individual to judge whether he or she was harmed by voluntary exposure to this free expression (e.g. in reading books) and not a matter of paternalistic judgment by the law. Neither the Report nor Beardsmore accept all of Mill's arguments. The Report, for example, is sceptical of Mill's optimistic opinion that in the 'free market' of ideas, good ideas will always multiply and bad ideas die out. Beardsmore in turn is critical of an 'empiricist assumption' at the heart of Mill's case, concerning the impossibility of attaining *certainty* in any of our judgments and *a fortiori* in our censorious judgments; he is also critical of Mill's handling of exceptions to the case against censorship.

Beardsmore himself offers a lively and provocative attack on *all* censorship of the arts (broadly conceived), not on the usual grounds of freedom of expression, artistic merit, uncertainty of harms or unsettled criteria of judgments, but because he sees an anomaly at the core of the institution of censorship:

> . . . it is necessary to the whole notion of protecting others from corruption which is central to any defence of censorship that the censor should refuse to judge his own moral beliefs in the same terms which he applies to those of others. He must . . . regard himself as in a better position to judge (Beardsmore, below, p. 104).

But, so Beardsmore argues, the very idea in moral matters of someone's 'being in a better position to judge' *makes no sense*. For one thing, it presupposes that there can be 'experts' in morality, rather in the way that there are experts in medicine or car-mechanics; this is an idea that Beardsmore rejects. Also,

> with moral issues . . . my judgment will count as a genuine moral judgment only insofar as it is not taken on trust but one which I have reached for myself (Beardsmore, below, p. 102).

This second point relates to Beardsmore's discussion of the case of children. Children should indeed, he thinks, be subject to protection but this cannot be called 'censorship'; 'it is coherent to speak of censorship only in respect of a person capable of reasoned judgment.'

Although Beardsmore pre-empts many of the issues about criteria raised in the Williams Report, there are points in the Report which have an interesting bearing on his argument. One concerns the idea of 'experts' in the field of morals and aesthetics. In the Report the idea comes up twice in the discussion (and rejection) of literary censorship. One of the final recommendations of the Report is that there be no restriction or prohibition on the printed word (they distinguish *written* from *pictorial* work, recommending the latter for various restrictions). Part of the authors' case against censoring the printed word is that there is no room for 'experts' here to judge, paternalistically, what is harmful:

> . . . questions on what one should read cannot be regarded just as questions of health, on which there are experts as there are experts on drug addiction, but are closely associated with questions of power and authority in society (*Report*, 5.27).

On similar grounds they reject the value, even coherence, of a 'public good defence' as a method of waiving supposed harmful effects by appeal to artistic or literary merit. They speak of the 'absurd model of the role of expert opinion with regard to artistic or literary merit'.

> The model is not so much elitist, as scholastic. . . . To assume that expert opinion is available at the event, that is to say at the time of publication, is merely to make the deathly assumption that all forms of artistic significance have already been recognized (*Report*, 8.23).

This criticism of the idea of the 'expert witness' does not imply a denial that aesthetic judgments, of the kind discussed by Olsen, can be made and sustained, for example, about pornographic works. The Report even offers some:

> Their participants are not characters, but mere locations of sexual possibilities; there is no plot, no development, no beginning, middle or end. . . . Moreover, since there are no characters or genuine human presence, the whole effect is dehumanizing . . . (*Report*, 8.12).

Such aesthetic judgments, though, never add up to a case for censorship.

Finally, it is worth noting the use Beardsmore makes of literary examples to support his argument against censorship. His discussion of Camus' *The Plague* is an integral part of his analysis of the nature of moral problems, an analysis designed to show that the idea of 'experts' in morality is inappropriate. Here is an overlap between philosophy and literature quite different from the philosophical concern with critical theory. Literary works can be powerful instruments in the exploration of philosophical problems, particularly in ethics. Philosophers, like writers of novels, and sometimes in conjunction with them, examine moral possibilities and the limits of imagination and understanding.[36]

There are of course other topics concerned with the aesthetics of literature that are not examined in these essays. But the range of topics that are discussed gives a good idea of current philosophical interest in the theory of literature. When notions like meaning, appreciation, sincerity, emotion or fiction come up in literary theory or when claims are made about the concept of literature or the procedures of criticism, there is always a danger at least of misunderstanding, even of deep-rooted disagreement or conflict of presupposition. It is the task of literary aesthetics, as a philosophical enquiry, to bring these abstract and elusive ideas to the fore and to expose them to careful logical analysis with the hope of attaining, if not agreement, at least a clearer conception of the sources of disagreement. It is to this end that the essays in this collection are dedicated.

NOTES

1   Stein Haugom Olsen, *The Structure of Literary Understanding* (Cambridge, 1978), p. 5.

2   Cited and discussed in T Todorov, 'Language and Literature' in R Macksey and E Donato (eds), *The Structuralist Controversy: The Languages of Criticism and the Sciences of Man* (Baltimore, 1972), p. 125.

3   H G Widdowson, *Stylistics and the Teaching of Literature* (London, 1975), p. 6.

4   Several of these concepts come from Cleanth Brooks, *The Well-Wrought Urn* (London, rev. edn, 1968); other classic discussions of 'poetic' language, in the tradition of New Criticism, can be found in W Empson, *Seven Types of Ambiguity* (London, rev. edn, 1953), I A Richards, *The Philosophy of Rhetoric* (Oxford, 1936), W K Wimsatt, *The Verbal Icon* (Lexington, 1954) and W Nowottny, *The Language Poets Use* (London, 1962). See also Daniel Burke, *Notes on Literary Structure* (Washington, 1982).

5   Monroe C Beardsley, *Aesthetics: Problems in the Philosophy of Criticism* (New York, 1958), pp. 126–8.

6   Malcolm Bradbury, *Possibilities: Essays on the State of the Novel* (Oxford, 1973), p. 10.

7   S H Olsen, *The Structure of Literary Understanding* (Cambridge, 1978), pp. 10–16; see also S H Olsen, 'What is Poetics?', *Philosophical Quarterly*, vol. 26 (1976) and S H Olsen, 'Defining a Literary Work', *Journal of Aesthetics and Art Criticism*, vol. 35 (1976–7). Colin Lyas, 'The Semantic Definition of Literature', *Journal of Philosophy*, vol. 66 (1969).

8   Colin Lyas, 'The Semantic Definition of Literature', *Journal of Philosophy*, vol. 66 (1969), p. 83.

9   See Victor Erlich, *Russian Formalism: History-Doctrine* (The Hague, rev. edn, 1965), p. 183.

10   Paul L Garvin (ed.), *A Prague School Reader on Aesthetics, Literary Structure and Style* (Washington, 1964), pp. vii–viii; *cit.* David Lodge, *The Modes of Modern Writing* (London, 1977), p. 2.

11   David Lodge, *The Modes of Modern Writing* (London, 1977), p. 2.

12   I A Richards in *Principles of Literary Criticism* (London, 1924) draws a distinction between the *emotive* function of language in poetry and the *referential* function in science, ch. 34.

13   T Todorov, *Littérature et signification* (Paris, 1967), p. 49; *cit.* T Hawkes, *Structuralism and Semiotics* (London, 1977), p. 100.

14   Cf. Jonathan Culler, *Structuralist Poetics* (London, 1975), p. 128: 'Rather than say, for example, that literary texts are fictional, we might cite this as a convention of literary interpretation and say that to read a text as literature is to read it as fiction.'

15   David Lodge, *op. cit.* p. 8.

16   Richard Ohmann, 'Speech Acts and the Definition of Literature', *Philosophy and Rhetoric* vol. 4 (1971), p. 14; for a similar theory, expressed in terms of 'translocutionary acts', see Marcia Eaton, 'Art, Artifacts, and Intentions', *American Philosophical Quarterly*, vol. 6 (1969) and 'Good and Correct Interpretations of Literature', *Journal of Aesthetics and Art Criticism*, vol. 29 (1970).

17   See M C Beardsley, 'The Concept of Literature', in F Brady, J Palmer and M Price (eds), *Literary Theory and Structure* (New Haven and London, 1973); included is a discussion of Lyas' criticisms of the 'semantic definition'.

18   Monroe C Beardsley, *The Possibility of Criticism* (Detroit, 1970), p. 59.

19   For a recent, and interesting, philosophical discussion of the relation between authors and narrators, see N Wolterstorff, *Works and Worlds of Art* (Oxford, 1980), pp. 163–79.

20   From John Sturrock's essay on Roland Barthes in: John Sturrock (ed.), *Structuralism and Since* (Oxford, 1979), pp. 76–7.

21   For an argument by a literary critic that characters are 'abstractions', see the classic article by L C Knights, 'How Many Children Had Lady Macbeth?', in *Explorations* (Harmondsworth, 1946). Knights uses the point to criticise certain styles of Shakespearean criticism which he thinks deflect attention from the poetry towards idle speculation about the characters. New Critical polemic is no part of my own purpose.

22   For classic philosophical discussions of the truth-value of sentences about fictional characters, see: Gilbert Ryle, 'Imaginary Objects', *Proc. Arist. Soc.* suppl. vol. XII (1933), and M Macdonald, 'The Language of Fiction', *Proc. Arist. Soc.* suppl. vol. XXVII (1954); my own position is similar in certain respects to that of Ryle.

23   For further discussion of this distinction, see S H Olsen, 'Literary Aesthetics and Literary Practice', *Mind*, vol. XC (1981).

24   For a useful discussion of the idea in aesthetics of 'emergent' entities, see Joseph Margolis, *Art and Philosophy* (Brighton, 1980).

25   Cf. S H Olsen, 'What is Poetics?', *Philosophical Quarterly*, vol. 26 (1976).

26   See S H Olsen, 'Literary Aesthetics and Literary Practice', *Mind*, vol. XC (1981), p. 538.

27   A good example is John M Ellis, *The Theory of Literary Criticism: A Logical Analysis* (Berkeley and Los Angeles, 1974).

28   Jonathan Culler, *Structuralist Poetics* (London, 1975), pp. 123–4; for a discussion of literature in the context of 'semiotics' see Culler's *The Pursuit of Signs* (London and Henley, 1981).

29   S H Olsen, 'Do You Like Emma Woodhouse?', *Critical Quarterly*, vol. 19 (1977).

30   Cf. S H Olsen, *The Structure of Literary Understanding* (Cambridge, 1978), ch. 2.

31 M C Beardsley and W K Wimsatt, 'The Intentional Fallacy', *Sewanee Review*, vol. LIV (1946); reprinted, with other useful essays, in D Newton-de Molina (ed.), *On Literary Intention* (Edinburgh, 1976); see also S H Olsen, 'Authorial Intention', *British Journal of Aesthetics*, vol. 13 (1973).

32 P D Juhl, *Interpretation, An Essay in the Philosophy of Literary Criticism* (Princeton, 1980), p. 12.

33 Colin Lyas, 'Personal Qualities and the Intentional Fallacy' in *Philosophy and the Arts*, Royal Institute of Philosophy Lectures, vol. 6 (London, 1973), pp. 200–1.

34 Clive Bell, *Art* (London, 1931), pp. 20, 115.

35 *Report of the Committee on Obscenity and Film Censorship* HMSO (London, 1979), 5.1.

36 For good examples and discussions of this kind of interplay between philosophy and literature, see R W Beardsmore, 'The Limits of Imagination', *British Journal of Aesthetics*, vol. 20 (1980), and D Z Phillips, *Through a Darkening Glass* (Oxford, 1982).

II

THE RELEVANCE OF THE AUTHOR'S SINCERITY

Colin Lyas

There are those who clearly discount the possibility that the sincerity of an author might enter relevantly into a critical appreciation of that author's work. C S Lewis, for example, writes that the question of sincerity 'should be forever banished from criticism'.[1] Such a view, also advocated in various writings by Beardsley, Wimsatt, Brooks, Warren, Wellek and others, has been received doctrine in much twentieth-century theory of criticism. The view even now appears to be gaining further ground under the influence of structuralist and post-structuralist literary criticism. To be sure, those who assert the irrelevance of references to authorial sincerity have not been without opposition. In 1968 Donald Davie, for example, wrote:

> The question "Is the poet sincere?"—though it would continue to be asked by naive readers—was always an impertinent and illegitimate question. This was the view of poetry associated with the so-called New Criticism, and it is still the view of poetry taught in our university classrooms. Must we now abandon it? I think we must (*Encounter*, 1968, pp. 61-6).

My concern is that the changes that occur from time to time in the climate of opinion about the relevance of references by critics to the sincerity or insincerity of the creator of the literary work, as well as many other references to authors, occur for no wholly clear and cogent reasons. In what follows I ask about reasons. At the very least I hope to raise doubts about some of the arguments that have been offered for the elimination from criticism of references to sincerity. Before I turn to those arguments there are two clarificatory points.

First, the arguments against the relevance of references to sincerity that I consider come mainly from theoreticians, notably Monroe Beardsley, who have been influenced by the New Critics. Different kinds of arguments might well be offered by writers in the Structuralist and Post-Structuralist movements. Whether or not what I shall claim is at odds with the views of those writers as well as with those of the heirs of the New Criticism is not a matter that I shall have space to discuss.[2] At the very least, however, I hope to clarify the position that anyone who wishes to establish the irrelevance of authorial reference, including reference to authorial sincerity, will have to undermine.

17

Perhaps when it is clear what this position is, the folly of attempting to undermine it will be apparent.

Second, although I have taken sincerity as a topic, I have wider concerns in mind, namely the general question whether the author had the feelings, beliefs and attitudes expressed in his work. These are not always issues about the relevance of sincerity, but I hope nevertheless to throw light on them. Indeed I shall be content to have established the claim that *some* references to a creator who is detectably present in a work of literature are not obviously irrelevant to the criticism of that work.

I

That many influential theoreticians are opposed to reference by critics to authorial sincerity can, I hope, be taken for granted. What is less clear is the basis for this opposition. We can, however, by collating various passages, construct at least one argument.

The first premise, which to some at least will seem axiomatic, is that the task of the critic is to talk about the work of art itself. Beardsley writes:

> I will use the term "critical statement", very broadly, to refer to any statement about a work of art, that is, any statement about such objects as poems, paintings, plays, statues, symphonies (*Aesthetics: Problems in the Philosophy of Criticism*, p. 3; hereafter *Aesthetics*).

The second premise asserts that we can distinguish generally between talk about the artist and talk about the work itself. Consider here the following comment by Beardsley on a piece of criticism by Edmund Wilson:

> The clauses in italics are about the novel, the rest are about the novelist; and the paragraph passes from one to the other as though there were no change of subject. . . . (E)qually good examples of the shift back and forth could be found in numerous critics of all the arts (*Aesthetics*, p. 19).

and he later remarks (*ibid*, p. 460) that we must 'bear in mind the distinction between judging the creator and judging his creation'.

From the two premises I have identified the intermediate conclusion is drawn that the task of the critic is to talk about the work and not the artist, so that authorial reference of any sort signals a deviation into irrelevance.

Now, trivially, to refer to authorial sincerity and insincerity is to refer to the author of the literary work of art. Hence such references involve a deviation into irrelevance. And so we find Beardsley eventually asserting the following:

> SINCERITY. In order to be applied to aesthetic objects . . .this term would presumably have to be defined in terms of some sort of correspondence between the regional qualities of the work and the emotions of the artist at the time of creation. When it is so defined, its irrelevance to the value of the object itself is fairly plain, though of course insincerity might be taken as a ground of complaint about the artist (*Aesthetics*, p. 491).

In assessing this argument I shall not query the validity of the inferences it involves. If its premises are true, its conclusions may well follow. Nor do I wish here to query the claim that the task of the critic is to address him or herself to the work itself. That being so the weight of my comments must fall on the claim that there is a radical distinction between talking of the author of a work and talking about the work itself. I shall begin by trying to cast doubt on this claim.

To assume the logical distinctness of work and artist is to assume, for any property we care to name, that the question 'Is this a property of the work or a property of the artist?' has a determinate answer. For a large class of property terms, including some that are in regular use by critics, the question 'Are you talking about it, the work, or about its author?' has no clear answer. I have in mind here the properties referred to when we use such terms as, 'perceptive', 'sensitive', 'glib', 'emotionally mature', 'intelligent', 'pretentious' and, I am tempted to add, 'sincere'. Thus when in *The Rhetoric of Fiction*, Wayne Booth says of *Lady Chatterley's Lover* that it is pretentious, he is talking about the novel. But it seems equally true of Lawrence that he was there pretentious, and indeed had *he* not been so *the novel* would not have been pretentious. Again when Leavis in *The Great Tradition* talks of the emotional inadequacies shown in the handling of the character Maggie Tulliver the question whether the emotional immaturity is a defect in the novel or in the novelist admits no clear answer either way. The only thing that seems open to us here is to refer to an entity which is neither of these exclusively but which is best referred to in the hyphenated phrase, 'the-artist-in-the-work'. For the terms I have mentioned are used to signal the place where artist and work merge together.

If the foregoing remarks are correct the second premise of the argument I have sketched is false and that argument against the relevance of reference to sincerity and insincerity collapses.

Those who offer that argument are not without resource here and I will now sketch one very prominent line of defence against the remarks that I have just offered.

The difficulty posed by what we may call the 'personal qualities' for those who subscribe to the first 'anti-author' argument that I have outlined is that reference to these qualities, although involving a reference to the artist, seem *at the same time* to embody a reference to the work. It is here that we need to consider an important suggestion by Beardsley and Wimsatt:

> The meaning of a poem may certainly be a personal one, in the sense that a poem expresses a personality or state of soul. . . . But even a short lyric poem is dramatic, the response of a speaker . . . to a situation. . . . We ought to impute the thoughts and attitudes of the poem immediately to the dramatic speaker and if to the author at all, only by an act of biographical inference.[3]

This suggestion, which relies heavily on the notion of the mask or *persona* allows that personal qualities *are* features of the literary work of art. But the claim now is that these personal qualities are personal qualities of the *dramatic speaker* of the work who should not be identified by the critic with the author of the work.

It is worth noting that on this account the term 'sincere' is one that may be relevantly predicated of works by critics. The sincerity, however, is, in this case, the sincerity of the dramatic speaker and not of the author. Thus Beardsley writes:

> The relevant and deciding question is: what sort of evidence does he (sc. the critic, C. L.) offer for saying that the work is sincere. . . . If he goes on to say that a love poem is insincere because he has discovered a letter written by the poet at the same time he wrote the poem, privately confessing that he didn't really care for the young lady at all, then the critic is talking intentionalistically. If on the other hand, he points out that certain phrases in the poem suggest that the dramatic speaker is aware of his own hypocrisy, then the critic is talking *objectively*—that is, about the aesthetic object (*Aesthetics*, p. 29).

In assessing this kind of strategy for the personal quality attributions two conditions have to be borne in mind. First, Beardsley and others who invoke the notion of the dramatic speaker are looking for a bearer of the personal qualities of the work of art that is clearly not identifiable with the author. Second, the posited bearer must be the bearer of the qualities *of the work itself*. The difficulties in meeting both of these conditions simultaneously may be glimpsed if we take a clear example of a dramatic speaker and ask whether that dramatic speaker meets the two conditions that I have mentioned.

In Dickens' *Great Expectations* the dramatic speaker is Pip. Like any other person, imagined or real, he may exhibit the full range of personal merits and demerits. He may be insincere, pretentious, perceptive, witty and so forth. Now Pip certainly meets the first condition that I mentioned , that is, no one has a right to identify Pip with the author of the work. But Pip does not meet the second condition. For it is obvious that the personal qualities in fact possessed by Pip are not the personal qualities of *the work itself*. Where it is perceptive, sensitive and emotionally mature, Pip is not. This, then, leaves us with the question, who is the bearer of the personal qualities *of the novel*, for it is certainly not the dramatic speaker.

At this stage one is, rightly, inclined to identify in many, although not all, novels a controlling intelligence whose attitudes and judgments as revealed to us by the response to the world of the work just *is* the novel. The second condition is now met in that we *have* found a suitable bearer for the personal qualities of the work itself. But now we do not obviously meet the first condition, for it is now no longer obvious that we should not identify the controlling intelligence with the author. And if, as Beardsley and Wimsatt seem to suggest, the sincerity and other personal qualities that we find in the work belong to the controlling intelligence, then, since we have now no clear distinction between the controlling intelligence and the author, it is no longer obvious that the sincerity and other personal qualities to which we refer in the work are not those of the author.

Having reached this point, some who have argued the separability of author and work seem to give up. Wimsatt, for example, writes:

> What we meant in 1945 (*i.e.* in the article on the Intentional Fallacy—C. L.) . . . was that the closest one could ever get to the artist's meaning or intending mind outside his work would still be short of his *effective* intention or *operative* mind as it appears in the work itself and can be read from the work.[4]

Here the suggestion seems to have become that reference to the author is all right if the evidence in support of it is found in the work. But now, if some references to the author-in-the-work are permitted, premise two of the argument I am examining is abandoned and with it the argument in that form.

Although, to judge from the passage that I have quoted, Wimsatt apparently gave up the radical author:work distinction, Beardsley never seems to have done so. In *his* later writing one finds quite a different kind of reason given why we should not identify the controlling intelligence and the dramatic speaker and hence why we should not identify author and work.

II

Beardsley writes:

> Now clearly Conan Doyle's use of the word "I" in the Sherlock Holmes stories does not give this pronoun a reference to an actual person. . . . Why then must we assume that when Keats or Shelley uses the pronoun he is always referring to himself? If you write a "Happy Birthday" poem and hand it to someone on his birthday or send it under your own name, you are giving the poem a pragmatic context. If you write a love poem, . . . you are not giving the message a pragmatic context; it is from nobody to nobody, it is not addressed to, but rather overheard by the reader: and though you are the writer you are not the speaker (*Aesthetics*, pp. 239-40)

and:

> The so-called poetic use of language is not a real use but a make-believe use. A poem can of course be used in performing an illocutionary act—it may, for example, be enclosed in a box of candy or accompanied by a letter endorsing its sentiments. But the writing of a poem, as such, is not an illocutionary act; it is the creation of a fictional character performing a fictional illocutionary act (*The Possibility of Criticism*, p. 59)

and finally:

> It does not matter how sincerely the poet believes his doctrines, or how fondly he hopes to persuade others. If he goes about making speeches, writing letters and distributing textbooks, then he is indeed arguing. But if he embodies his doctrines in a discourse that flaunts its poetic form . . . and directs attention to itself as an object of rewarding scrutiny, then, so to speak, the illocutionary fuse is drawn. His utterance relinquishes its illocutionary force for aesthetic status and takes on the character of being an appearance or a show of living language use (*ibid.* p. 60).

The suggestion in these passages is that to concern oneself with the author of the work is to ignore what makes a literary work a literary work of art. This has to do with its being a clearly signalled kind of pretence, an act of imaginative creation, an invention or play of the mind that is not to be trammelled with considerations about what the author really thought or felt. Such a claim has a long history and if it is true we have some reason for distinguishing the author and the, possibly pretended, controlling intelligence in the work. Moreover, whether or not a general distinction exists between author and work, we would, if the 'pretence' view is true have a presumption against the relevance in criticism of references *to sincerity*. For questions of sincerity arise only where there is no unfettered license to pretend to views, feelings and attitudes that one does not have. If such unfettered licence *is* granted to the author as literary artist, then questions of sincerity and insincerity would seem not to arise when the work is considered as *art*.

I have introduced the 'pretence' or 'imitation' view as outlined by Beardsley in the context of the claim that there is a general distinction between talking of the artist and talking about the work of art. Against that claim I argued that the personal quality terms we use of works of art resist the effort to make this distinction; the controlling intelligence in the work to whom these terms apply is logically indistinguishable from the author. The pretence view rebuts that suggestion. For since the author may be pretending to be the controlling intelligence of the work we have no licence as critics to identify him or her with the controlling intelligence of the work. I now wish to indicate why this line of approach fails.

To begin with, the notions of 'imitation' or 'pretence' invoked by Beardsley are limited both by what it is possible for a pretender to pretend and what it makes sense for an audience to assume is being pretended. Now with respect to many of the personal qualities that we attribute to the controlling intelligence of a work it makes little sense to assume that an author could pretend to possess them when he in fact does not. If the kind of quality of response shown by the controlling intelligence of a work, and hence by the work itself, is perceptive, sensitive, emotionally mature and the like, there seems to be little sense in the supposition that the artist has, by an act of pretence, embodied these characteristics in a work although he himself was not possessed of them. The judgment that the work *is* these things is the judgment that the author *there* exhibited those qualities (though he might not otherwise exhibit them in the responses of his or her non-literary life).

There are, then, logical limits on what might be successfully pretended. What complicates matters is that though it looks odd, in the case of *meritorious* personal quality features of works, to say that there is successful pretence to merit qualities not possessed, nevertheless, for the *demeritorious* features pretence does seem possible. A writer can produce a work in which he or she successfully pretends to an insensitivity, glibness and mawkishness that is far from his or her true character.

In certain contexts, e.g. pulp fiction writing for profit, this activity of pretence makes sense. But although there is in strict logic no impossibility in this, there are doubts as to whether it can rationally be supposed by readers of putative *works of art* that this kind of pretence is going on. Take again here *The Mill on the Floss*. Leavis has observed, rightly to my mind, that there is an inadequacy in the characterisation of Maggie Tulliver. He writes:

> We are most likely to make with conscious critical intent the comment that in George Eliot's presentment of Maggie there is an element of self idealisation. The criticism sharpens itself when we say that with the self idealisation there goes an

element of self pity. George Eliot's attitude to her own immaturity as represented by Maggie is the reverse of a mature one.[5]

Here a critic has attributed demeritorious qualities to a controlling intelligence. But the suggestion that we should not assume, as Leavis does, that these are demerits of the author, on the grounds that some kind of pretence might be going on, seems not rationally sustainable. True, that supposition might make sense if we were dealing with pulp fiction, but here we are dealing with what purports to be a literary work of art. The intention in creating such a work is the intention to create an object of value and it would be self contradictory, granted this intention, to attempt to fulfil the task by creating a bad work, e.g. one that is mawkish, glib, pretentious and the like.

One other thing is worth noting in this context. Those who have argued for the pretence or imitation account of art have failed to distinguish carefully enough *what* is imaginatively pretended even in works of fiction, where their account most naturally applies. What is imaginatively presented to us in a fictional work is the world of the work. That is conveyed to us in a series of explicit and implicit pseudo-assertions which do seem like imitations of real assertings. But where there is *in* such works a valuational response to the world of the work (as in many cases there is) then although *the world* to which there is a response is pretended, *the response* is not. Here the controlling intelligence of the work is not a character in the fiction. So some works of fiction really are, in Marianne Moore's famous image, imaginary gardens with real toads in them.

The effort to create a general distinction between the controlling intelligence and the author seems to fail, and since that distinction is required if there is to be a general distinction between talking about the artist and talking about the work, that distinction fails too and with it the general argument against the relevance of references to sincerity with which I began. I turn now to a somewhat different line of argument.

III

Again the argument begins with the claim that the task of the critic is to talk about features of the work itself. In the light of what has just been said, however, to this cannot now be added the *general* claim that to refer to the author *at all* is to deviate from the task of talking about the work. If, though, we had a proof that authorial *sincerity* is not a feature of the work itself, then we could get to the conclusion that references to authorial sincerity are irrelevant to the proper task of criticism, even though other kinds of authorial reference might not be.

One kind of argument goes something like this: if something genuinely is a property of an object then its possession by that thing must be ascertainable solely by scrutiny of that thing. Now, on Beardsley's account, if I am to know that a work is sincere, I need to know something that the work itself cannot tell me, namely that the author actually had the feelings, attitudes and beliefs that the work expresses. Hence sincerity is not really a property of the work and so the critic can ignore it.

One reply to this line of argument would be to argue that the work itself can give us evidence that the author or artist did have the feelings, attitudes and beliefs expressed in the work. As I have just argued, the self pity expressed in the characterisation of Maggie Tulliver in *The Mill on the Floss*, though detectable only from the work, seems indistinguishable from some kind of failing in the work's author. And writers have perfectly good ways of making it clear to us, by their titles, by nudges in the text, that they do or do not wish to be taken as expressing their own responses. (Consider here Swift's *Modest Proposal*.)

That reply, however, does not touch upon the substantial drawback to the proposal, namely the suspect epistemological status of the assertion about what it is for a property *really* to be a property of a thing. (Indeed, as it stands the proposal merely begs the question against those who wish to claim that sincerity *is* really a property of a work, even though we may need background knowledge in order to predicate it of the work itself.) What it is for something really to be a property of a thing is indeed a problem in philosophy, as discussions of the so-called Cambridge changes amply illustrates.[6] As a contribution to the solution of that problem the proposal before us seems far too strong. That a piece of wood is a chess knight, that a killing is murder, that an object is a work of art are all facts, knowledge of which requires more than mere scrutiny of some object or action. But from that it will not follow that in discovering these facts we are not discovering things which are *really* true of objects and actions, or that we are discovering things that are not really essential to the proper description of actions and things.

We should note in this connection the oddity of saying, with respect to sincerity, that since we need an assumption about a person before we can say that what that person has written or said is sincere, so the judgment that it is sincere or insincere is a judgment, as Beardsley puts it (*Aesthetics*, p. 491) about the artist and not about the object. But to the contrary, 'sincerity' seems to function like the personal quality terms that I mentioned earlier. If, on receiving her poem, Marvell's coy mistress had said, 'This *is* insincere', the question, 'Are you talking about the poem or about Marvell?' looks odd. Whether or not what she said was relevant to art appreciation, she was, in a hyphenated phrase, talking about the-author-as-shown-in-the-work. True, a matter to which I come shortly, she could have said, 'It *looks* insincere, I wonder if he meant it?', just as we can say, 'It sounds sad, I wonder if the composer was?' But that a work can look insincere (or sad) when its creator is not, does not establish that it itself cannot *be* sincere or insincere; nor does it establish the falsity of the claim that when it *is* either of these, it is what it is because its *author* is *there* sincere or insincere.

The general claim that the only real properties of a thing are those detectable solely by scrutiny of it is no basis for the dismissal of sincerity as a property of the work itself, and hence as a critically relevant property. But although there is ample evidence that some would like to see sincerity off as irrelevant in this way, behind these considerations there lurks a quite different argument, one based on the claim that whether or not sincerity is a feature of the work itself it is not an *art-relevant* feature. I turn now to efforts to make this third kind of argument stick.

IV

We have come now to an argument the first premise of which is that the critic should be interested only in the art-relevant features of a work. The second premise will be that sincerity, and possibly the other personal qualities that I have mentioned, are not art-relevant features.

In order to carry conviction with those who are inclined to refer to sincerity in talking of art this second premise must be more than merely asserted. (Sometimes it is merely asserted. When Ortega y Gasset asserts that 'preoccupation with the human contents of a work is in principle incompatible with aesthetic enjoyment proper' and when Bell says 'to appreciate a work of art we need bring with us nothing from life' no reasons appear.[7]) More interesting here are the tactics of those who seek to restrict what is relevant to the appreciation of art to features that can be identified solely by scrutiny of the work itself without the need of any background or contextual knowledge. This way of thinking underlies what Wollheim has felicitously called 'The Presentational Theory', the theory, as he puts it in *Art and its Objects* (para. 24), 'that a work of art possesses those properties, and only those, which we can directly perceive or which are immediately given'. There is ample evidence that Beardsley is inclined this way:

> I propose to count as characteristics of an aesthetic object *no* characteristics of its presentations that depend upon knowledge of their causal conditions, whether physical or psychological (*Aesthetics*, p. 52).

Now there is some licence for Beardsley's view in the fact that often when we refer to aesthetic features we are referring to the surface perceptual qualities of a thing. But from this two things do not follow. First it does not follow that the only kind of interest that we want to call an aesthetic interest is an interest in the surface perceptual qualities of a thing. Hence it does not follow that an interest in sincerity, let alone an interest in some of the other personal qualities that I have mentioned, is not an aesthetic interest. Second, even if the aesthetic qualities of a thing were its surface perceptual features, it will not follow that seeing those features requires no background of knowledge and experience, so that anyone, even one with the empty cognitive stock to which Kant referred, could see the aesthetic features just by looking. The fact that something is an aesthetic feature does not analytically rule out the possible need for background knowledge and experience, and if this is so, it is not obvious that *sincerity* can be ruled out as irrelevant because it requires background knowledge.

But suppose it were true that aesthetic features were none other than the surface perceptual features and that to perceive these in a work required no pre-existent body of knowledge, it would now be trivially true that judgments that a work is sincere would not be aesthetic judgments. But now we need some demonstration that aesthetic judgments, in the sense defined, are the only critically relevant judgments of a work of art. Here, first, it is not clear to me what argument is offered for this contention and, second, critics appear anxious to deny it. Leavis, for example, writes:

> When we examine the formal perfection of *Emma* we find that it can be appreciated only in terms of the moral preoccupations that characterise the novelist's peculiar interest in life. Those who suppose it to be an 'aesthetic matter', a beauty of 'composition' can give no adequate reason for the view that *Emma* is a great novel.[8]

Without a demonstration that literary works of art are important as art solely by virtue of their surface perceptual features, it is not clear why the fact that works have these art-relevant surface properties shows the irrelevance of critical references to their other properties such as their sincerity. The same comment goes for another attempt to rule considerations of sincerity out on the grounds that it is not a surface property. If I understand him correctly Alan Tormey has suggested that the term 'expression' has two employments.[9] Sometimes we may say that a face wears a sad expression, sometimes we may say that it expresses sadness. In the former case to know that the face is sad is to know how it looks, regardless of whether its owner is in fact sad. In the latter case to know that the face is sad is to know that the person whose face it is, is sad. Tormey, it seems, believes that when we say that a work of art is expressive, *e.g.* is sad, we are, so to speak, saying something about its 'looks'.

If this account were true it would bear in two ways on the question of the relevance of sincerity. First, to say that a work is sincere or insincere would be to say that it has a sincere or insincere *look* about it ('rings' true or false, as we sometimes say). And then the sincerity or insincerity of the work to which we refer in criticism would have nothing to do with *authorial* sincerity. Second, there is an oblique argument against sincerity. For to say that a work *is* sincere might seem to refer to the fact that it expresses what its *author* feels or believes. Its sadness, for example, is his. But on the Tormey account the expressive features of the work are not those of the artist, and so the question of the sincerity of *his* act of expression does not arise for critics of the work.

Again this account is likely to seem arbitrary to one inclined to refer to the author's sincerity. Granted that to take an interest in expressiveness in art is to take an interest in the 'look on its face' rather than whether it *is* really sad or sincere, then it will follow that we are not interested in whether *its author* is sad or sincere. But one who is tempted to refer to authorial sincerity will want to know *why* he should grant the assumption underlying this line of approach. Tormey, it seems to me, is well aware of this difficulty and it is to his answer that I now turn.

Tormey writes:

> And if my style of playing poker expresses my temerity or my avarice, why should not my style of painting landscapes express something of me as well? Or my style of playing the flute? The conditions of a warranted inference to an intentional state may as well be met by art as by action. . . . It is this sense in which I concede

that an art work may be an expression of something: it may contribute material leading to a correct inference to an intentional state of the artist. But I contend that this . . . does nothing to distinguish art from any other product of human activity (*ibid.* pp. 117–18)

One difficulty with the passage is the reference to 'inference'. For it does not seem to me that when a person's poker playing expresses something of his personality that I *infer* his personality from the playing. Rather I directly see it in the playing, just as in the earlier case I have mentioned we might see directly in the fine details of *The Mill on the Floss* character deficiencies of the controlling intelligence expressed *there*. Moreover, if I find that Cowper, to take one example, did not feel the sentiments expressed in the lines *To Mary* I do not *infer* that the lines are insincere—rather that is how I see them. However, this is not the chief interest of the passage. That lies in the suggestion that if we do treat the work as expressing its author's feelings and attitudes then we might lose sight of what makes art *art*. It is here that I find the crucial weaknesses of the case against the relevance of references to sincerity. In the remarks that follow I shall attempt to rebut the suggestion that something in the nature of art makes it impossible to take a relevant interest in the fact that the feelings, attitudes and beliefs expressed in the work are those of the artist.

V

The claim is then that we are forced by our interest in the work of literature as a work of art into treating its expressiveness as a surface perceptual feature. Like the look on the face of a bloodhound, the sadness of the surface of an art work is not connected necessarily to any inner sorrow of its creator.

No reason seems to me to be given, as yet, why what we might call 'real expressions' *cannot* be art. Indeed since such works as Picasso's *Guernica*, Goya's war paintings and Solzhenitsyn's *The Gulag Archipelago* seem to be both works of art *and* real expressions, it may well not seem obvious that this is so. We need, then, a demonstration why, because of the nature of art, the critic cannot take an interest in the 'real expressiveness' of a work.

Two of the reasons that Tormey suggests seem to me not to have great force. First, he writes:

The expressionist theorist is committed to the . . . assumption of a necessary link between the qualities of the art work and certain states of the artist. Critics of this theory have been quick to observe that this would commit us to treating all art works as autobiographical revelations (*ibid.* p. 104)

But first, I cannot see the need to commit oneself to the view that *all* works are autobiographical revelations in order to maintain that *sometimes* an interest in the work as a real expression is compatible with an interest in it as art. I am not obliged to treat imaginative thought experiments, like Yeats' *An Irish Airman Forsees his Death* as I might treat Cowper's *The Castaway*.

Second, even if I am obliged to treat all works as autobiographical revelations the passage quoted does not tell me why this is incompatible with treating them as art.

Another of Tormey's considerations is expressed thus:

> 'That's a sad piece of music' is countered not by objections such as, 'No, he wasn't' or 'He was just pretending' (referring to the composer), but by remarking 'You haven't listened carefully' or 'You must listen again; there are almost no minor progressions and the tempo is *allegro moderato*' (*ibid.* p. 105).

This is unconvincing for two reasons. To begin with, although 'He was just pretending' may be an odd and seemingly irrelevant reply to 'This piece of music is sad', it is not obviously irrelevant as a reply to the assertion 'Henry King's *Exequy* is sad'. What the point of saying this might be I come to later, but if the claim is only that remarks about art which signal that we are treating expressive works as real expressions always sound odd, then my example challenges that. Next, 'This music is sad' does indeed seem to me to translate into 'This music sounds sad', and whether the composer is or is not sad may be as irrelevant to that claim as the internal states of the bloodhound are irrelevant to judgments about the cast of its countenance. But for this to be an argument against expression theorists Tormey needs a demonstration that the way a work sounds or looks is the only art-relevant thing about it. For if remarks like, '*Guernica* expresses Picasso's reaction to the bombing of a village' are art-relevant, remarks like 'He was only pretending' are no longer odd. Tormey's present argument, therefore, presupposes that treating a work as a real expression is incompatible with treating it as art, whereas what we were looking for are reasons for believing that that is so.

One other aspect of Tormey's treatment is worth mentioning since it enables me to reinforce some earlier remarks. Tormey quotes a programme note on Nielsen's Sixth Symphony which refers to the second movement as 'a bitter commentary on the musical modernism of the 1920's'. Tormey then writes:

> the prevailing impression left by the music itself is that of lighthearted buffoonery. It may not be unreasonable . . . to conclude that Nielsen was venting exasperation, bitterness or disappointment here, but it is difficult to see how such an inference could have been suggested by attending to the qualities of the music alone. The music does not *sound* exasperated or disappointed, nor can I see how any piece of music *could* have these as perceptible qualities. . . . The suggestion that Nielsen was manifesting exasperation or commenting bitterly on musical modernism in this piece can have arisen only with the acquisition of some extra-musical information about the composer's life. If the critic now wants to maintain that the Sixth Symphony is an expression of Nielsen's bitterness and disappointment, we may agree that this is at least a plausible inference given the truth of the biographical data. But we must also point out that this has little to do with the aesthetically relevant expressive qualities of the music itself (*ibid.* p. 109).

Now there may be difficulties in hearing disappointment and bitterness in a piece of music if we have no knowledge of its provenance. But from that it does not follow, first, that it is equally difficult to detect these in other art forms, e.g. painting and literature. Think here of Swift's *Verses on the Death of Doctor Swift*. Further, from the fact that we need background knowledge in order to say that a piece of music is bitter, it does not follow that bitterness is not really a property *of the music*, nor that it is not an art-relevant property. All that follows is that bitterness is not an immediately perceptible surface feature. But again, although there is a strong suggestion in the passage that these surface features are the only art-relevant ones, there is no *argument* for this 'aestheticist' conclusion.

The stage we have reached is this: failing any obvious argument that sincerity is not really a property of a work of art, we are driven to asking whether it is an art-relevant property. What Tormey seems to have shown is that sincerity is not a certain kind of art-relevant property, namely, a surface perceptual aesthetic feature. But that is not enough to show that sincerity is not an art-relevant property at all. I turn now to another attempt to show the art-irrelevance of sincerity.

VI

Let us at this point return to Beardsley's remarks on art and imitation. The central feature of this view is the claim that to create what we call art is intentionally to engage in a clearly signalled kind of pretence to be a character with certain beliefs, feelings or attitudes. The truth in this view is that authors are at liberty to produce, and frequently have produced, 'imitations' of this sort, as when Yeats articulates the thoughts of an Irish airman who foresees his death or Tennyson writes as if Ulysses. Now sincerity and insincerity seem not to be considerations where there is a licence to pretend, and the artist seems to have that licence. If art is authorised pretence there may seem as little sense in asking if the author was sincere as in asking Olivier whether *he* really felt suicidal when playing Hamlet.

This whole approach depends on the truth of the claim that to create art is intentionally to engage in a clearly signalled imitation, so that the creator becomes a kind of actor. There are problems with this. To begin with, even if it is true that to create art is to engage in imitation it does not follow that reference to the artist himself (and possibly to his sincerity) is thereby eliminated. Although what is imitated is not real, imitation is a real act and as such is open to the kinds of personalistic appraisals that all acts are open to. In particular imitation is often undertaken for a purpose. The artist wishes, through the creation of a fictionalised world, presented to us in imitations of real assertions, to articulate a response to that world or to make a comment through it (as Orwell does in *Animal Farm*). To judge that response is to judge the author, and his response to the fiction is not a fictional response.

Even if the pretence view is generally true, then, we are not done with the artist. The real problem is, however, that it is not generally true that all works of art are imitations. Some, like Tennyson's *Ulysses* are (although even here there seems to be a comment that is not imitative). Some works are clearly not like this. Henry King's *Exequy*, and Peter Porter's echo of it, do not merely pretend to a grief, they express a grief that was felt (as, in different contexts, do such works as Picasso's *Guernica* and Elgar's *Cello Concerto*). Hence it seems flatly false that to create a work of art is to engage deliberately in a clearly signalled act of pretence. Consider here Henry Miller's reply to the critic who suggested that Miller *ironically* adopted the pose of the all-American bum:

> The theme is myself and the narrator, or the hero as your critic puts it, is also myself . . . if he means the narrator, then it is me . . . I don't use heroes incidentally, nor do I write novels. I am the hero, the book is myself.[10]

And in another place Mary MacCarthy writes that 'the whole point of this story was that it really happened; it is written in the first person; I speak of myself'.[11]

Now it is open to Beardsley to say that whether or not a work of literature is pretended, if we are to treat it as art we should treat it *as* we treat a legitimate form of pretence, that is with no regard to whether or not the pretender's feelings correspond to those that are pretended.

There is a drawback to this. For the suggestion only makes sense if the notion of treating all works of literary art (whether or not they are imitations) as imitations is a coherent one. But it is not. It is not a coherent option because we are interested in imitative art for special reasons. To take *that* kind of interest in an imitative work, however, we must know that it *is* actually an imitation. If it is not, and we know that it is not, there is a peculiar pointlessness in trying to treat the work as an imitation. By way of illustration consider the following case.

Switching on the radio I hear what I take to be the song of the nightingale. As I listen I enjoy the aesthetic quality of the sounds. An announcer then says, 'Thank you Percy Edwards'. The situation is now changed. Though I do not withdraw my aesthetic appraisals, a whole new range of appreciative terms becomes appropriate, terms in which I assess the imitation as such.

There will be those who will claim that the appraisal here is of Percy Edwards and not of the sounds that I heard. I hope in view of what I have said earlier that it is not obvious that wedges can so easily be driven between producer and product. There will be those, too, who will say that the appraisal of the imitation is not as aesthetically relevant as my appraisal of the original notes. That seems to me to ignore the fact that, as Aristotle was the first to notice, there is a basic human delight in imitation, depiction and the like. Part of this delight is the delight of the unfettered imagination as we co-operate in the pretence. Part of it has to do with a delight in watching the free play of the creative intellect. Whatever the analysis of the matter, we do delight in fiction, imitation and representation and have terms in which to appraise them for their plausibility, verisimilitude and the like. These appraisals may fall in a different category from our appraisals of the qualities of mere sounds, but they are part of the form of life that is constituted by the varied pattern of our interests in art. To exclude them from the critical reckoning reflects mere prejudice in favour of the surface perceptual features of works.

If we are to show an interest in a work of the kind we show towards imitations, and if we are to apply to it the categories of appraisal we reserve for imitations, we must know, or be able reasonably to assume, that that is what it is. If, for whatever reason, we know that it is not an imitation, it is impossible to take an interest in it as such and indeed it might be perverse or even tasteless to try and do so. It would, for example, be perverse to treat Swift's *Modest Proposal* as one might treat an imitation of outrage, pretended as an aesthetic feat, by one who felt no anger, and it seems tasteless to treat such poems as Cowper's *The Castaway* in this way.

I cannot, then, see the sense in saying that we should treat literary works of art as imitations, even if they are not. What, apart from a desire to eliminate authorial reference, would be the point of that? But even if it did make sense to treat all non-imitative works of literature as imitations, so ignoring the fact that they are real expressions, we still need an argument *why* we should do so. Until we have such an argument we have no justification for the view that the critic can dispense with references to authorial expression. I turn now to another consideration that seems to suggest itself to many.

VII

Let us recall here the remark of Tormey that if we take an interest in the work of art as a real expression of its author's feelings there is 'nothing to distinguish art from any other product of human activity' (*ibid.* p. 118). This suggests the following kind of worry; since many things that are real expressions are not art, to study the work as a real expression is not to study it as art. Or, to put it another way, being a real expression is not what makes a thing art, so that aspect of the matter can be ignored when the work is treated *as* a work of art.

This is a very weak argument. Consider the following analogy. Many things that are beautiful are not art; hence beauty is not what makes a thing art and so that aspect can be ignored when a thing is studied *as* art.

Now if we feel that the status of a thing as art is not impugned when we attend to such features as grace, beauty, elegance and balance, which are also features of things that are not art, it becomes obscure why a thing's status as art should be impugned merely because we attend to a real expressiveness that some works of art share with things that are not art, or because we refer to a sincerity or insincerity that things other than works of art may display.

The truth of the matter seems to be that a merit or demerit becomes a merit or demerit of art when it is predicated of a thing that has on other grounds the status of art. Trivially art-merits are merits found in art and the fact that the same kinds of merits are valued in other things does not undermine their status as art-merits when they occur in art. To be sure there will be the problem of saying what it is for something to be a work of art, but that will not show the falsity of the view that a merit can be an art-merit even if it is a merit of other things that are not art. Hence the fact that sincerity and insincerity are features of things that are not art does not establish that they cannot be features of art.

There is a further aspect of this matter. When we take a merit or demerit term that is used in non-artistic contexts and apply it to art, we should not expect the rules governing its use to change. This is important since it allows me to deal with a misunderstanding about the use of the terms 'sincere' and 'insincere' in artistic contexts. I have heard it said that sincerity cannot be an important consideration in art because the fact that a person sincerely believes the beliefs and feels the feelings he or she expresses in a work of art will not necessarily lead us to think more highly of the work. This, however, assumes that those who think sincerity is important in art are obliged to think that sincerity is automatically *merit conferring*. But in at least one important sense of the term 'sincere' (see § IX below) this is not even true of sincerity in its non-artistic manifestations. Someone who sincerely believes that Slavs are sub-human is not in any way excused because he sincerely believes this. Hence, if one believes that sincerity is a relevant consideration in art one is not obliged to believe in the simplistic inference that runs, 'This is sincere, therefore this is good.' What one *is* required to think is a matter to which I now turn.

VIII

So far I have found no compelling reason why reference to the sincerity or insincerity of a work is critically irrelevant. That invites the following response. 'At best your arguments show that no good reason has been given for the elimination of critical references to sincerity, or, more generally, for the elimination of references to the fact that the work is really expressive. This does not give any ground for believing that such references *are* relevant. What *positive* arguments are there then?' I shall now say something about this, pausing only to remark that it may be no small achievement to have established the negative case and thus to have undermined the settled assumption that it is obvious that considerations about sincerity are irrelevant in criticism.

Let us take first a feature of art that seems unproblematic, say elegance. If I am asked why elegance is an art-relevant property, granted it *is* something we value in things other than art, I seem to have no reply other than it is something that we do find interesting and important generally and that our interest in it continues when we find it in art. My inability to give an analysis of the term 'elegant' or to say why we find it important in life and in art does not hinder my right to say that it *is* an art-relevant property. That is established by the fact that as well as finding this property important in non-artistic contexts we also find it important in art. That in turn is shown by our paying attention to it, finding it worth remarking on there. Now by parity of reasoning I should like to say that if people do find sincerity and insincerity worth remarking on in art, and, more generally, if they find it worth noticing that the work is a real expression, that establishes the art-relevance of these things.

That leaves two possible questions that might be asked. One is 'Do people in fact mind about sincerity and insincerity in art?' and the other is 'Why do they?'. As to the first I wish to claim that where a clear intimation of the imitative status of a work is absent we are interested in whether it *does* express the attitudes, beliefs and feelings of its creator. We are interested, first, in whether these are adequately expressed, and we use terms like 'mawkish', 'pretentious', 'sensitive', 'mature', 'intelligent' and a host of others to express our estimation of this. In addition we are interested in the fact *that* beliefs, attitudes and feelings of a work, where there is no evidence that these are pretended, *are* the beliefs, attitudes and feelings of its creator. If we discovered that Pasternak did not have the kinds of attitudes expressed by the controlling intelligence of *Dr Zhivago*, or that Solzehnitsyn did not have those expressed in *The Gulag Archipelago* this would not be a matter of indifference.

I note here that even a cursory survey of critical writing will establish the claims that I am making. Critic after critic refers to what this or that *artist* did, to the quality of the response of *the author*. So natural and ubiquitous are such references that even those critics who in terms of their theories should avoid them, unhesitatingly and with no sense of strain in fact make such references in their practical criticism. Thus Cleanth Brooks, dubbed by Beardsley a 'poem reader' and not a 'mind reader' can write:

> In using logic, Donne as a poet is fighting the devil with fire. . . . In other words the poet wishes to indicate that his vision has been earned, that it can survive reference to the complexities and contradictions of experience.[12]

Given the kind of evidence to which I have referred we can say, parodying a famous modern slogan, that reference to the artist is part of the 'form of life' that criticism takes. As such there is at least a presumption in favour of it and the onus is on those who object to such references to find positive reasons for their elimination. Hence the importance of the negative parts of this paper in which I have tried to show the paucity of such reasons.

That leaves the question why sincerity and insincerity matter in art. I am not sure that I need to answer this granted that we do find it important in art. I need only say that we find them important considerations in art for the same reason we find them important in life, whatever that is. But although I need not do so I would like to say a little more than this about sincerity and insincerity in art.

IX

One problem here is that we have no very good analysis of the concept of sincerity in its non-artistic manifestations. This lack inevitably affects a proper understanding of the role of judgments of sincerity and insincerity in our judgments of art.

That aside, the first point I would make here is that in art, as much as in life, it is not so much a question of our finding sincerity a positive good as a case of our feeling *in*sincerity to be something bad. Sincerity may be of importance not because sincerity is good in itself but because it signals the absence of something positively bad, namely *in*sincerity. But why then do we disvalue insincerity? The following are tentative suggestions.

Speaking very broadly it seems to me that we can distinguish at least two uses of the term 'insincere'. (These two uses may be related and it would be a nice task to show this.) First, it is not unusual to find the term 'insincere' used (and Leavis[13] so uses it) of poems like the following where, we might say, the 'cringe quotient' is somewhere around force nine:

> Man proposes, God in his time disposes,
> And so I wandered up to where you lay,
> A little rose among the little roses,
> And no more dead than they.

> It seemed your childish feet were tired of straying,
> You did not greet me from your flower strewn bed,
> Yet still I knew that you were only playing,
> Playing at being dead.

> I might have thought that you were really sleeping,
> So quiet lay your eyelids to the sky,
> So still your hair, but surely you were peeping,
> And so I did not cry.

> God knows, and in His proper time disposes,
> And so I smiled and gently called your name,
> Added my rose to your sweet heap of roses,
> And left you to your game.[14]

The problem here is not that the person speaking lacks the feelings expressed or that the poem does not express them adequately. Rather there is a sense of something wrong with feeling that way and, consequently, with a poem that articulates that way of feeling. (Note how the attitude changes if we know that this is an academic exercise in the mawkish. We now might enjoy the poem. But note how that enjoyment depends on a knowledge of provenance and authorial intention.)

Whether or not insincerity is the best term to use of such a poem (it is after all deeply felt), this term *is* used and signals the fact that we are interested in the quality of expressed feeling. Why we *are* thus interested, by what criteria we judge this quality and to what end we make these judgments is unclear to me, and until these matters are clear we will be unclear about the place of insincerity, in this sense, in our judgments about art. The fact is, however, that there does seem to be something wrong with the quoted poem and that 'insincere' is critically used to say what is wrong. So are terms like 'mawkish', 'pretentious', 'slushy' and the like. This being so there is no real problem about insincerity, granted what I have said earlier. 'Insincere', like 'mawkish' and 'sensitive', becomes one of the class of personal quality terms that, so I have argued, apply to qualities shown by an author-in-a-work.

The second sense in which we use the term 'insincere' is to express our belief that an illegitimate pretence to feeling is going on. Why does *this* matter? For it does. Some at least of us could not be indifferent to a discovery that Picasso did not care about Guernica. Here again I offer a tentative suggestion.

I earlier suggested that there might be a division made between purely imitative imaginative works (like Yeats' *Irish Airman* ...) and the non-imitative, e.g. Cowper's poem *To Mary* or King's *Exequy*. And there are works which, although fictional, are essentially non-imitative in that the author purports at least to express his real attitude via the fiction.

The most that a purely imaginative work can tell me is how someone, e.g. an Irish airman, *might* respond to something, e.g. his impending death. In judging this work I judge its *plausibility*, relying on my *pre-existent* knowledge of human nature. The work does not add to that pre-existent store. It teaches me nothing new, save in the sense that it reveals to me possibilities inherent in what I already know about human beings. (The knowledge imparted to me is like the 'knowledge' imparted to me by the possibly surprising conclusion of a geometrical proof.) In a non-imitative work, however, I am, if the work is genuine, told not how someone *might have* responded, but how someone *did* actually respond. This *adds* to my knowledge of the functioning of human beings. (Imitative art, we might say, stands to the non-imitative, as mathematical stands to empirical knowledge.)

Non-imitative art adds to my empirical knowledge of human nature. This is why we are unable to be indifferent when we discover that what we took to be sincere expression of an actual emotion is not so (though there need be no deception here). What I thought to be an addition to my store of empirical knowledge about human beings (knowledge in which I have an interest *as* a human being) turns out not to be so, and at the very least a different kind of response is called for. At best I have to move now from considerations of truth to considerations of plausibility.

It is because what is believed to be a non-imitative work is likely to be taken as expressing its author's attitude that devices have been found for signalling to the audience that a work is *not* of that sort, e.g. by, sometimes ironical, indications in the title or by nudges in the work itself. Where these are absent we are entitled to assume, although the assumption is defeasible, that a real response is beng articulated. So, too, we have sometimes the author's anxiety to establish, as Brooks puts it, that his vision has been earned and tested in the fires of experience.

Something of what I have said may explain some of our unease when confronted with evidence of insincerity and other forms of duplicity in art. But I have no doubt the matter goes deeper than this, as deep indeed as our notion of sincerity goes. We will not understand why we would be disturbed if we found that Solzehnitsyn did not have the attitudes expressed by *The Gulag Archipelago* until we know why we care that someone we took to be a close friend was planted on us as a spy.

X

Two 'master thoughts' have governed this paper. One is the notion that in the last resort the answer to the question, 'What is relevant in the criticism of art?' is determined by what human beings find interesting and important in art. I have claimed that many do take an interest in real expression, including many who in theory should not. And then, in the absence of a proof that that interest is incompatible with criticism, all we can do is say 'This game is played'. True it may turn out that there *is* an incompatibility here, but if the negative part of my paper is right, we have not yet found it. There will, of course, be those who object to these Wittgensteinian ways. To defend the methodology would, however, take me beyond this paper.

The second 'master thought' is that a work of art *inter* (very much) *alia* records for us the complex response of a real person to a situation, real or imagined. In *it*, given the requisite knowledge and experience, we can see the chronicle of choices made, of temptations avoided or succumbed to and of attitudes expressed. *Some* works are like this and for them we can judge the controlling intelligence and so the work in terms of the adequacy of the chronicled response. We can do this even if we have no biographical knowledge of the author.

When we make this judgment of the controlling intelligence we do not *infer* to a mind existing independently of the work; we see a mind in action *in* the work. Although to see this may require sensitive scrutiny of the fine details of the writing. Judgments of the mind operative in the work are as much judgments of *it* as judgments of its surface perceptual features.

My view that the work is a response does not exclude an interest in its other aspects. One may study the phonetic cadences and the reverberations of poetic tropes. One may study the way in which the work is extruded from the author by the social and other pressures of his milieu and the way in which its expression is tempered by structures inherent in language and culture. Unless, however, we have a demonstration that the individual personality of the author makes no contribution at all, the worthiness of these other objects of study does not rule out an interest as well in the creator's performance, registered in the work, as he mediates between the forces of his culture and the constraints of his language.

NOTES

1   E M W Tillyard and C S Lewis, *The Personal Heresy* (Oxford, 1965), p. 120.

2   I discuss this matter in a forthcoming issue of *RESTANT* devoted to the work of Monroe C Beardsley.

3   M C Beardsley and W K Wimsatt, 'The Intentional Fallacy', in D Newton de Molina (ed.) *On Literary Intention* (Edinburgh, 1976), p. 2.

4   W K Wimsatt, 'Genesis: a fallacy revisited', in Newton de Molina, *op. cit.*, p. 136.

5   F R Leavis, *The Great Tradition* (Harmondsworth, 1962), p. 54.

6   See, e.g. P T Geach, *God and the Soul* (London, 1969), p. 71 f.

7   See my 'The Dehumanisation of Art', *British Journal of Aesthetics*, vol. 13, (1973).

8   *op. cit.* p. 17.

9   A Tormey, *The Concept of Expression* (Princeton, 1971).

10   Reported in Edmund Wilson, *The Shores of Light* (London, 1952), p. 70.

11 'Settling the Colonel's Hash', *Harper's*, February 1954, pp. 68–75.
12 *The Well Wrought Urn* (New York, 1947), but see the preface to the 1968 edition.
13 See the essay, which is Leavis *fortissimo*, 'Reality and Sincerity', *Scrutiny*, vol. 19.
14 I regret that I cannot supply the author. I take the example from an exercise in unseen appreciation, à *la* Richards, which I had to do many years ago at school.

III

CRITICISM AND APPRECIATION

Stein Haugom Olsen

I

Consider the following description (the undergraduates' description) of Aeschylus' *Agamemnon*:

> ... the watchman appears, sees the signal fires which mean that Troy has fallen, utters a dark hint or two, and disappears forever from the play. The Chorus enters and offers, by way of entertainment, a history of the Trojan war, with a long special appendix on the sacrifice of Iphigenia. Clytemnestra enters and interprets the signal fires quite correctly; and the Chorus refuses to believe her, apparently on no better ground than that she is merely a woman. A herald comes in, tells them the same thing, and they believe him (he, you see, is a *man*). The play is half over before Agamemnon appears. He becomes immediately involved in an argument with Clytemnestra over the interesting question of whether he will or will not walk on the red carpets which she has spread for him. He proves conclusively that he ought not to, and then does walk on them after all, of course, for he is a married man. ... Cassandra finally speaks, and we have one of the greatest failures of communication in history. Presently, from off-stage, Agamemnon gives us a blow-by-blow account of his own murder. And that is pretty much that.[1]

This is a parodic presentation of what is in fact an 'undergraduate understanding' of Aeschylus' play. It is obviously inadequate, not merely because it is synoptic but because it fails to provide any concepts which could be used to illuminate the different scenes to which it refers. Take the description of the carpet-scene. It is concise and includes references to the most important phases of the scene. But if one sees nothing further in the scene than what this description includes, one misses its point totally and utterly. A more adequate understanding of the scene could be expressed in some such description as the following (the professor's description):

When Agamemnon is about to enter, the chorus sings an ode where it recapitulates 'yet again the progress of the Trojan War and the dark moral lessons which it has taught'.[2] The chorus in this ode also introduces the theme that 'Evil fathers bring up evil children', thus associating with Agamemnon and his actions the maxim that 'crime breeds crime'. This association is part of a pattern of references to 'Agamemnon's crimes' and 'retribution' which has occurred in proximity in the choral songs from the beginning of the play. Thus when Agamemnon enters, it is 'into an oppressive atmosphere of guilt and evil, for we have not been allowed to forget for a moment the chain of events which has led this unhappy family to this point'.[3] The past for the House of Atreus is a sequence of black and bloody deeds: the murder of Thyestes' children, Agamemnon's sacrifice of Iphigenia, the sacking of Troy. And when Clytemnestra rolls out the purple carpet and the debate starts between her and Agamemnon about whether or not he should walk on it, this background of associations is firmly in place. The carpet itself is not only the occasion for and the subject of the debate. It adds significantly to the atmosphere of foreboding. For its colour, purple,

> was not the reddish-blue colour which we know today, but a reddish-brown, since the dye used to produce this shade included in its composition the blood of a mollusc, the *murex* or purple-fish. It is in fact that brownish-red which is the colour of congealed blood ("blood spilt on the ground", "dark" blood, is one of the major images throughout the trilogy), and it provides a brilliant visual symbol. For, out of the main doors in the proscenium—which has, throughout, represented the House of Atreus—there curls out towards us this long stream of blood, seeping out of the house. . . . Aeschylus thus creates a marvellously theatrical way of translating into visual terms that idea which he has been pressing insistently throughout the play, the blood of the Atreidae: Thyestes' children, Iphigenia. As soon as Agamemnon steps on to the carpet he is sealed with that blood, blood which he has himself helped to spill.[4]

When the carpet is rolled out, the contest between Agamemnon and Clytemnestra then focuses one of the major themes of the play: the perversion of the natural order which has manifested itself not only in the father (Agamemnon) killing his daughter to procure fair weather for the Greek fleet on its way to Troy, and in the unnatural extirpation of even the seeds of life in Troy and the blasphemous destruction of the Trojan sacred shrines, but also in the usurpation by a woman of the man's place in the House of Atreus. It is the latter which is brought to a climax in the carpet-scene. It is quite correct to say that Agamemnon 'proves conclusively that he ought not to walk on the carpets and then does walk on them after all'. Doing this he accepts honours reserved for the gods only and thus he shows *hubris*, but much more important is the fact that he yields to Clytemnestra. In yielding to her and thus setting aside his own reasoned opposition to her suggestion, he accepts her dominance: Clytemnestra unmans him. Subjecting Agamemnon, Clytemnestra takes over his role and makes it permanently her own. Agamemnon bows out of the contest, yields Clytemnestra the victory and steps into the stream of blood seeping out of the House of Atreus. His blood is added to that of Thyestes' children and to that of Iphigenia.

It was suggested above that the professor's description of the carpet-scene expresses a more adequate *understanding* of the scene than the under-graduates' description. I now want to improve on this suggestion. For these two descriptions do not represent merely two different levels of sophistication in the understanding of *Agamemnon* as a literary work. They constitute *criteria for two qualitatively different pay-offs* from the play. The professor's description of the play *defines an experience* which is richer than and superior to the experience defined by the undergraduates' description.

The type of interpretative description of a literary work which these two descriptions represent defines a degree of a type of value, and the authors of the undergraduates' description consequently differ from the author of the professor's description in their evaluation of the work. The undergraduates experienced *Agamemnon*, as they experienced Greek tragedy in general, as 'interesting but primitive' and they were unwilling to grant the play greatness as a literary work.[5] On the other hand, for the professor it was an unequivocally great play:

> No apologies need be offered for the *Oresteia*, no concessions to those who hold Greek tragedy to be unapproachable or irrecoverable. Its dramatic impact will never be weakened by time; it continues to live in the theatre, as modern performances in many languages have shown; and it continues to challenge scholarship and criticism to do justice to its astonishing richness.[6]

The primitiveness which the undergraduates complain about in *Agamemnon* is mirrored in their description of the play which is poor in detail, mentioning only a few main features, and which is also lacking completely in interpretative characterisations of the features mentioned. The dramatic impact and richness which the professor experiences, is defined by his description which is both rich in detail and in interpretative characterisations.

II

Rather than say that the two descriptions represent different levels of sophistication in the understanding of *Agamemnon*, I would suggest that they define different levels of *appreciation* of the play. The undergraduates' description and the professor's description of *Agamemnon* define a type of experience going beyond a mere act of understanding. And it goes beyond a mere act of understanding by being an experience of value: the descriptions define a degree of a type of value. However, it would be inaccurate to say that this experience goes beyond mere understanding by being understanding-cum-value judgment. For the descriptions of the carpet-scene in *Agamemnon* do not involve value judgments. They constitute reasons for the value judgments made by their authors, but they do not themselves contain any evaluative terms nor any statements which could be construed as making the description an implicit evaluation. While they define what one could metaphorically call the reader's perception of the work and while this perception is the perception of a degree of value, the description does not add up to a statement about the degree of value perceived.

Consider now a different case: the appreciation of wine. Appreciation of wine involves a sensation of taste which constitutes the *recognition* of the features which make the wine an object of appreciation, as well as the *experience* which makes this recognition into a case of appreciation. Appreciation of wine can be more or less adequate, and its adequacy depends on the adequacy and correctness of the *discrimination* involved, on how far the taster succeeds in identifying the features which make the wine worthy of appreciation. A discriminating palate is identified by its ability to distinguish good wine from bad wine, different types of wine from one another, i.e. the ability to identify the genesis of the wine (vintage and area), and by its ability to characterise the taste of a wine in a suitable vocabulary, metaphorical and literal. Inadequate appreciation is characterised by lack of discrimination, i.e. failure to determine the character of the taste of the wine. Good wine is sought by discriminating palates for its taste: the taste of wine is, for discriminating palates, an experience of a degree of value. The degree of value is identified by determining the quality of the taste, i.e. through discrimination. Appreciation of wine, involving the sensation of taste, is obviously different from a mere act of understanding, and the nature of the experience involved is clear. However, the connection between the discrimination of the qualities of taste and the experience of value is necessary: the discrimination of the qualities of the taste constitutes the experience. There is, finally, agreement about what is more or less adequate and correct discrimination, and about what is discrimination as opposed to other types of judgment, say, an attempt to determine the acidity of wine. That is, there is agreement about what types of judgment constitute discrimination. This agreement is of a peculiar type. It is an agreement on the level of the senses which cannot be formulated in a general rule stating what is correct and adequate discrimination. But the agreement is not merely a matter of spontaneous, shared perception. The agreement is *brought about* through a cultivation and education of taste. The untrained palate is never a discriminating palate. In the appreciation of wine there is thus a standard involved. The standard is not in the nature of a rule; it is not a principle which can be formulated but is constituted by the authoritative judgment of those who are presumptively qualified to judge. A difference in opinion about what is correct discrimination can be settled only with reference to the pronouncement of qualified judges. There is no appeal procedure when those acknowledged as supreme authorities disagree. Such a fundamental disagreement would represent a crisis for the community of wine connoisseurs, threatening the coherence of the standards shared by its members and thus threatening the very concept of a community of connoisseurs defined by common standards.

In the appreciation of wine discrimination is exclusively perceptual. Discrimination is literally an exercise of taste and the cultivation of taste increases one's ability to perceive, to recognise nuances and qualities previously not perceived at all. Consider now yet another case of appreciation, the appreciation of scenic beauty:

Edward returned to them with fresh admiration of the surrounding country; in his walk to the village, he had seen many parts of the valley to advantage; and the village itself, in a much higher situation than the cottage, afforded a general view of the whole, which exceedingly pleased him. This was a subject which ensured Marianne's attention, and she was beginning to describe her own admiration of these scenes, and to question him more minutely on the objects that had particularly struck him, when Edward interrupted her by saying, "You must not inquire too far, Marianne—remember I have no knowledge in the picturesque, and

I shall offend you by my ignorance and want of taste if we come to particulars. I shall call hills steep, which ought to be bold; surfaces strange and uncouth, which ought to be irregular and rugged; and distant objects out of sight, which ought only to be indistinct through the soft medium of a hazy atmosphere. You must be satisfied with such admiration as I can honestly give."[7]

Edward Ferrars sees exactly the same scenery as Marianne Dashwood. They can both identify each single feature in the scene without disagreement. Yet Edward excuses himself because of his 'ignorance and want of taste' and Elinor Dashwood says about him that 'he affects greater indifference and less discrimination . . . than he possesses'.[8] For in the appreciation of scenic beauty discrimination is not purely a matter of perception. Somebody who wants to appreciate scenic beauty must not only identify the features of a scene, but must also recognise these features as what makes the scene worthy of appreciation, as aesthetic features. And this involves a judgment, an aesthetic judgment, going beyond mere perception. When Edward confesses 'ignorance and want of taste' he does not mean that his powers of perception are deficient, but that he lacks *sensibility*: the ability to go beyond perception and recognise the aesthetically valuable features. Edward's self-proclaimed inability to appreciate scenic beauty is not an inability to recognise the features of the scene, but an inability to recognise their beauty or ugliness. In this respect there is a significant difference between the appreciation of wine and the appreciation of scenic beauty. However, appreciation of scenic beauty is just like appreciation of wine in that it is different from an act of understanding. It involves the experience of a degree of value, i.e. of beauty or ugliness as well as the recognition of visual features. This experience of beauty or ugliness is defined through discrimination: the identification of such features as constitute the beauty or. ugliness of the scene. In the absence of this experience there is no appreciation, though one perceives the very same features. The features are there for all to see but an act of appreciation is required to see their beauty. Appreciation of wine and appreciation of scenic beauty also share the feature that the discrimination they involve is governed by standards of adequacy and correctness. However, there is a difference between the contexts in which judgments about wine and judgments about scenic beauty are made which must have consequences for the kind of standard involved in the two cases. Appreciation of wine is a communal activity and what is adequate and correct discrimination is determined by a community of connoisseurs. The discriminating palate is the palate trained to make the discriminations which the community makes. This communal context is absent in the appreciation of scenic beauty. There is no community of connoisseurs determining what is adequate and correct aesthetic description of a scene. It can be made clear to every aesthetically sensitive person whether an aesthetic description is or is not correct and adequate, and aesthetic sensibility is not the result of an initiation into the values of a particular limited group.

The distinctive features of these two types of appreciation is that they involve discrimination, that through discrimination is defined an experience of value which goes beyond a mere act of understanding, and that discrimination is subject to standards of adequacy and correctness. It is a measure of the adequacy of discrimination how far the identification of such features as make the object worthy of appreciation is carried.

III

With the concepts and insights provided by the discussion of these two types of appreciation, it is possible to clarify and develop the suggestion that the undergraduates' description and the professor's description of *Agamemnon* represent different levels of appreciation of the play rather than attempts to understand it. The notion of discrimination can be introduced into the characterisation of these descriptions by help of a distinction between textual and aesthetic features. A textual feature is a feature of style, content or structure. These are features possessed by all texts. All texts have phonological, syntactic, semantic and a minimum of rhetorical features. All texts have a content which can be described in various ways; and all texts structure their content and their formal features in some way. Textual features can be identified by everybody who masters the language in which the text is written. Aesthetic features, on the other hand, are what constitutes a text a literary work. They are identified through an aesthetic judgment and though they are made up of bundles of textual features, they cannot be reduced to textual features. Textual features are analogous to visual features which are seen and recognised without the exercise of sensibility. Aesthetic features are analogous to such features as are identified in discrimination by the exercise of sensibility. They are the type of feature which makes an object worthy of appreciation and they can only be identified in appreciation. Discrimination, as represented by the undergraduates' description and the professor's description, involves two basic, inter-related judgments. In discrimination textual features are identified as aesthetically important or significant. This is done in an interpretative judgment which assigns to the textual feature its significance. There are not two independent judgments here, i.e. first an identification of a textual feature and then an interpretation of it. The interpretation determines the very nature of the textual feature. In the professor's description of the carpet-scene in *Agamemnon* the colour of the carpet is singled out for attention through an interpretative description which both fixes the character of the colour (it is the colour of congealed blood) and the role of the carpet in the artistic vision which Aeschylus builds up for us. Now another description of the carpet-scene ignores the colour and concentrates instead on the economic implications of the carpet: 'The tapestries are precious; a lot of work has gone into them.' The dye used to colour them is difficult to extract and it requires skill and hard work to embroider them. When Agamemnon refuses to tread on the carpet, it is due to these economic considerations: he does not want 'to waste the substance of the *oikos*'.[9] In this interpretation the actual colour of the carpet is of no significance. What matters is the investment it represents. Thus, in discrimination, a textual feature (the colour of the carpet) has to be assigned an aesthetic function (being a symbol of the Atreidian blood) if it is to appear as a textual feature relevant to *Agamemnon* as a work of art.

Discrimination is more or less adequate according to what extent it provides interpretative descriptions of textual features. The undergraduates' description of the carpet-scene in *Agamemnon* is a mere summary of content:

> The play is half over before Agamemnon appears. He becomes immediately involved in an argument with Clytemnestra over the interesting question of whether he will or will not walk on the red carpets which she has spread for him. He proves conclusively that he ought not to, and then does walk on them after all, of course, for he is a married man.

The red carpet is mentioned, that is all. The professor, on the other hand, identifies the carpet as a symbol of the spilt Atreidian blood. He takes the carpet out of the immediate context provided for it and constructs a new context linking it to other elements of the play, to Thyestes' children, the sacrifice of Iphigenia, Agamemnon's imminent death. He provides a rationale for this scene by placing the carpet as part of a meaningful pattern. He exercises his aesthetic discrimination just as Marianne Dashwood exercises her sensibility and sees a 'bold' hill where Edward Ferrars sees only a 'steep' one, surfaces 'irregular and rugged' where Edward sees only 'surfaces strange and uncouth'.

Discrimination, being the identification of textual features as aesthetic features in an interpretative description, is necessarily concerned with specific textual features, and it is a further measure of the adequacy of discrimination that it maximises the number of textual features successfully assigned aesthetic significance. The professor's description contrasts with the undergraduates' description not merely in that it provides interpretative descriptions of the textual features it mentions, but also in the respect that it is more sensitive to what is actually in the text. The professor's description mentions more features of the scene and describes the character of these features. Thus, discrimination in literary appreciation, just like appreciation of wine and scenic beauty, is a way of apprehending phenomenally the object of appreciation. And in discrimination the peculiar and unique character of the literary work is brought out.

Discrimination in the appreciation of wine is purely perceptual: a recognition of a quality of taste. Discrimination in the appreciation of scenic beauty goes beyond mere perception and involves a judgment about a quality emerging, in some way, from the combination of visual features for those with sufficient sensibility. It is easily recognised that appreciation of wine and scenic beauty involves, through discrimination, an experience which is its point: the taste of a good wine and the view of scenic beauty are their own rewards. Now even if it is granted that the undergraduates' description and the professor's description involve a type of judgment analogous to discrimination, this type of judgment is different, in one important respect, from discrimination as it is exercised in the appreciation of wine and scenic beauty: it is exclusively intellectual. Aesthetic features are identified not in perception through the exercise of literal or metaphorical taste, but in an interpretative description through the application of a set of concepts and conventions. There is no perceptual experience involved here which is obviously its own reward, and there is thus a difficulty in this case for the suggestion that the two descriptions of *Agamemnon* define a type of experience going beyond the act of understanding.

The fact, noted above, that the descriptions of *Agamemnon* can be used as reasons for value judgments by their authors does not, in itself, distinguish them from other descriptions which obviously do not define an experience beyond the act of understanding. A test-report on a camera will describe those features of it which are relevant to its performance and durability: the resolution of the lens; its light-transmitting ability; the way the lens is mounted on and released from the body; the features of the viewfinder; the method of focusing; the shutter: its material, the way it works, its reliability, its performance in extreme temperatures; the lightmeter: its sensitivity and accuracy; the range of accessories available and the ease with which they are mounted and changed; the material and design of the camerabody itself, etc. This description expresses an understanding of the features which make the camera a good one, and it can be used as a basis for an evaluative judgment: whether or not the camera is a good buy. But this description is not its own reward, as it would be if it constituted appreciation. A test-report is written to guide buyers or makers of a product, not for its own sake.

The suggestion that the professor's description and the undergraduates' description each define an experience of a degree of value which goes beyond mere understanding can, however, be supported by the following considerations. The descriptions of *Agamemnon* do not point beyond themselves. They are their own ends. They do not figure as premises guiding action. They can be used as reasons for value judgments about the play, but such value judgments do not assert the excellence (or lack of it) of the play in serving some function other than that of having such features or combination of features as the description identifies. In a lens, high resolution is a feature of excellence because it results in sharp pictures. The carpet as a symbol of the Atreidian blood in *Agamemnon* is a feature of excellence because it contributes, and because of the way in which it contributes, to the definition of the artistic vision presented in *Agamemnon*, not because it promotes some further purpose served by the play.

Furthermore, the undergraduates' description and the professor's description do not constitute a stage in a theoretical explanation of the play, as does the following description of the 'To-morrow'—lines in *Macbeth*:

> To-morrow, and to-morrow, and to-morrow,
> Creeps in this petty pace from day to day,
> To the last syllable of recorded time;
> And all our yesterdays have lighted fools
> The way to dusty death. Out, out, brief candle!
> Life's but a walking shadow; a poor player,
> That struts and frets his hour upon the stage,

And then is heard no more; it is a tale
Told by an idiot, full of sound and fury,
Signifying nothing.

In effect, the unconscious content leads me to bed for the night, a kind of regression, and prepares me for imaginings. Curiously, though, that shift from going to bed to the stage-play is accompanied by a shift from visual images (the candle, the walking shadow) to aural: a strutting and fretting which is *heard* no more, a tale full of *sound* and fury which signifies nothing. There is thus also a shift from the direct experience of life—the immediacy of "Creeps" and "Out, out"—to merely being told about something. Similarly, the days of the first five lines give way to night, a night vivid but at the same time distanced as a dream, stage-play, or tale, a night, in other words, of imaginings. There is still a third shift in the imagery: the day was associated with creeping or a syllable, rudimentary skills, while the night is marked by complex adult activities, telling a tale or play-acting.

The images act out a going to bed followed by frightening imaginings associated with adult activities, namely, a stage-play. Psychoanalysis deals with subjective states; generalisations are therefore difficult. Nevertheless, there is a well-documented and well-nigh universal unconscious meaning to dreams and fantasies of watching stage performances: they signify a child's fantasies of watching what he takes to be the sadistic, bloody violence of his parents in the struggle of love ending in a death-like sleep. So the poem ends in the blankness of "no more", "nothing". So, too, the poem distances the stage-play as sound rather than sight. Similarly, the phrase, "Out, out, brief candle", becomes ambiguous if we consider possible phallic symbolism: it may be a command to withdraw the penis concealed in the sexual act or detumescent after. "Walking" distances sexual activity into another kind of erect action.

In short, if we translate the poem into terms of impulse and defense, the impulse is bifold: to see but not to see that exciting but frightening performance. The poem defends against the wish to see by distancing the performance into sound, "a tale" to be "heard", and it symbolises the watched sexual act into a more or less respectable adult activity: watching a play.[10]

This description resembles the professor's description in the following respect: it mentions many textual features and assigns to them interpretative descriptions. And the identification of textual features is always through an interpretative description. However, it differs from the professor's description in that it represents a stage in a theoretical explanation of a presumed effect which the passage in question has on readers. According to the theory in question, the reader will register this effect without being able to give *or even to understand* the interpretative description given by this critic. The critic thinks he has observed that the 'To-morrow'—passage 'stands out over all the others as a set piece to be mouthed in the beardless lips and cracked tenors of thousands of adolescents whom teachers will make memorise it. It is the one speech in *Macbeth* which every actor must dread, for his audience will lean over collectively to its neighbor and to show his erudition, whisper the first three lines.'[11] The reason for the fame of this passage is the emotional impact it has: 'To me, the passage brings a tremendous feeling of reassurance and peace, admittedly a gloomy sort of peace, but peace nevertheless.' The *cause* of this reaction is, according to this critic, to be found in the latent fantasy-content of the passage, and this fantasy-content can be recovered by help of psychoanalytic theory. The quoted description identifies textual features by help of concepts and conventions dictated by this theory. According to psychoanalytic theory, says this critic, 'there is a well-documented and well-nigh universal unconscious meaning to dreams and fantasies of watching stage performances: they signify a child's fantasies of watching what he takes to be the sadistic, bloody violence of his parents in the struggle of love ending in a death-like sleep'. So the references in the passage to 'player' and 'stage' determine what fantasy to look for; psychoanalytic theory also offers a generalisation about the attitude of every human mind to the situation which is the object of fantasy, and consequently all the elements of the passage are interpreted in the light of these results of psychoanalytic theorising. The professor's description of *Agamemnon* does not stand in the same relationship to a general theory of literature, the human mind, or society, as does this description. The concepts and conventions it uses are not derived from any general theory, nor does it explain in the way that the description of the 'To-morrow'—passage does. While the psychoanalytic explanation is not concerned with the valuable experience itself, only with its *cause*, the professor's description is concerned with defining and expanding the valuable experience itself. The fact that the descriptions of *Agamemnon* do not point beyond themselves, i.e. do not figure as premises for action or as a stage in a theoretical explanation, together with the fact that there is an obvious analogy between discrimination as it occurs in the appreciation of wine and scenic beauty and in these descriptions, strongly suggests that these descriptions do define an experience of a degree of value which is its own reward. If they did not it would be impossible to give a rationale for these descriptions. Adequate interpretation such as the professor's description represents a considerable intellectual effort. It is the fruit of years of training and weeks or months of reading and reflection. There must be a legitimate reason for this effort. Furthermore, though the descriptions do not figure as premises for action, they do figure as premises for value judgments, and if what is judged is not the quality of an experience, then this feature of these descriptions will be unintelligible.

IV

Discrimination in the appreciation of wine and scenic beauty is subject to standards of correctness and adequacy; standards which also define appreciation as a special type of judgment. Now it seems intuitively obvious that the professor's description is more adequate than the undergraduates' description, and that the professor's description, adequate as it is, might be challenged as incorrect, if it could be shown it errs with regard to the factual information of which it makes use (it might be mistaken in the inference that the colour of the carpet is that of congealed blood) or if it could be shown that some of its interpretative descriptions are less plausible than those offered by a different interpretation (there may be reasons for preferring the description of the carpet as a symbol of wealth, the economic substance of the *oikos*, to the description of the carpet as a symbol of the Atreidian blood). In the light of the preceding discussion it also seems reasonable to assume that the descriptions of *Agamemnon* can be construed as expressing judgments of a distinctive type, different from all other types of judgment which can be made about the play. So the question whether there is an analogy between appreciation of wine and scenic beauty, on the one hand, and, on the other, the descriptions of *Agamemnon* also in the respect that they all are based on the characteristic standards of adequacy and correctness, has an obviously positive answer. The answer is not very telling. It gives no new information about the character of literary appreciation. However, the question whether literary appreciation is governed by standards leads necessarily to the more interesting and important question concerning the nature of these standards and thus to the question concerning the logical status of literary appreciation *vis-à-vis* other types of judgments about literary works.

In the appreciation of wine and scenic beauty the standards for correct and adequate discrimination are constituted by the authoritative judgment of those presumptively qualified to judge. In the appreciation of wine those presumptively qualified to judge are the trained connoisseurs; in the appreciation of scenic beauty it is those endowed with the right kind of sensibility. Discrimination in literary appreciation is constituted by the identification of textual features as aesthetic features through the application of interpretative descriptions. Neither literal taste nor sensibility to emergent perceptual features can figure in the definition of the standards for correct and adequate discrimination in literary appreciation. A judgment concerning the adequacy and correctness of discrimination in literary appreciation is supported by reasons. For the present purpose it will be useful to draw a rough distinction between two types of reasons. There are reasons which appeal to what one may call the natural rationality of a reader: they will be understood and accepted by every rational creature who speaks the language in which the work is written. Perspicuity, consistency, and correctness are required of any description which is to fulfil its purpose in the best possible manner. However, the reasons that were used when it was explained above in what way the professor's description is more adequate than the undergraduates' description are not of this type. The reasons were that the professor's description distinguishes many more textual features and aspects of textual features than does the undergraduates' description and that it not only mentions textual features but also provides interpretative descriptions for them. Now the whole operation of identifying aesthetic features, of identifying textual features as having a function other than the one they have as textual features, may seem 'natural' to any trained reader, but it is a highly sophisticated operation involving both concepts and conventions which have to be *learnt* before it is possible to appreciate *Agamemnon*. The significant difference between the undergraduates and the professor is not that the undergraduates are less rational than the professor but that the undergraduates are at the beginning of a learning-process which the professor has gone through. The professor's appreciation of *Agamemnon* involves the application of a set of concepts and conventions and it is these concepts and conventions which define the standards of adequacy and correctness and also the distinguishing features of the type of judgment constituting literary appreciation. Until these concepts and conventions are mastered, appreciation of *Agamemnon* is impossible. Appreciation of a literary work does not come naturally. It is a cultural phenomenon and is, in this respect, analogous to the appreciation of wine rather than to the appreciation of scenic beauty (though one should not make too much of this contrast, since nothing has been said about the nature of sensibility). It is a *non-natural* mode of apprehension distinct from both a pragmatic and theoretical perspective. It is not, of course, an *un*-natural mode of apprehension. For if it is correct to construe the appreciation of *Agamemnon* as governed by a set of concepts and conventions, then the existence of these concepts and conventions *provides a possibility of offering Agamemnon* as an object of appreciation. And for these concepts and conventions to have a continuing function, there must be people regularly producing texts for appreciation as well as readers employing these concepts in appreciation. If no texts were produced with the intention that they be appreciated as literary works, then literary appreciation of texts would have only an incidental interest and the concepts and conventions defining appreciation would quickly fall into disuse. To appreciate *Agamemnon* as a literary work is to assume that it has been intended for and therefore will yield to appreciation. Appreciation is assumed to be the *correct* way of apprehending *Agamemnon*.

These last remarks imply an answer to the question concerning the logical status of appreciation *vis-à-vis* other types of judgment about literary works. If there is a practice constituted by authors producing works for aesthetic appreciation by readers, then appreciation has a privileged logical status among the types of judgment which concern literary works. The features making a text a literary work are identified in discrimination. Thus they exist only in appreciation, and all types of judgment concerning literary works other than appreciation (ignoring the problem of second-order judgments, i.e. judgments based on appreciation but going beyond it)[12] must be construed as judgments about aspects of a text, as judgments about textual features, rather than as judgments about literary works. The psychoanalytic explanation of the 'To-morrow'—lines in *Macbeth*—whether one accepts it or not—does not involve discrimination: a description of those features which make the passage an integral part of the literary work *Macbeth*, and which confer on the passage literary value. Consequently, the psychoanalytic explanation must be admitted to have only incidental relevance for the reader interested in the literary function of the passage. For this explanation is concerned with features of some latent content of the text and such a latent content can be found in *any* text: a description of a dream, a joke, any piece of imaginative prose, in essays, etc. Only in so far as such a latent content can be seen *in discrimination* to constitute a feature of the *literary work Macbeth*, is the identification of it relevant to a reader interested in *Macbeth* as a literary work.

That the psychoanalytic explanation of *Macbeth* is different in kind from the professor's description of *Agamemnon*, can be revealed through an analysis which requires no more than common sense. The kind of judgment constituting appreciation, on the one hand, and, on the other, judgments of mere understanding are mutually independent. Once the logic of appreciation has been made clear and it has been contrasted to judgments of mere understanding, no further arguments can be given in support of the claim that appreciation has a privileged logical status among judgments concerning literary works. That the judgments presented in the professor's description of *Agamemnon* have a privileged logical status in relation to the object of description which the judgments presented in the psychoanalytic explanation of *Macbeth* lack, can only be recognised by somebody who knows the practice, who knows not merely what texts are labelled 'literary works', but who can also appreciate them as such. Common sense is not here enough. The present argument has been just such an attempt to clarify the logic of appreciation, to appeal to the reader's implicit knowledge of how to deal with literary works, and to make him see the way in which he deals with literary works as part of a practice.

V

The term 'literary criticism' is used to refer to all types of comment on literature. It has not been the purpose of this paper to suggest that only some types of comment constitute genuine criticism while other types of criticism are spurious. There is no reason to legislate against any types of comment on literature. What is important from the point of view of literary aesthetics is to recognise if there is a type of judgment expressed in such comments which is constitutive of a reader's view of a text as a literary work. This will necessarily involve the deflation of the claims to explain literature made by most types of theoretical criticism, e.g. psychoanalytic criticism, Marxist criticism, structuralist criticism, archetype-criticism, etc. Clearly, this may lead one to question the point of such criticism as involves the use of these theories and to conclude that this criticism really serves no purpose. However, there is no legislation involved. In fact, appreciation can occur under many different labels and it can be intertwined with many other types of judgment. Appreciation is not a type of criticism but a mode of apprehension. An analysis of appreciation does not provided a basis for legislating about criticism but is a way of identifying that core in criticism which is constitutive of our concept of literature.

NOTES

1 Elder Olson, *Tragedy and the Theory of Drama* (Detroit, 1961), p. 5.
2 Brian Vickers, *Towards Greek Tragedy* (London, 1973), p. 362; the following description is built on Vickers' argument.
3 *Ibid.* p. 364.
4 *Ibid.* pp. 366-7.
5 Elder Olson, *op. cit.* p. 4.
6 Brian Vickers, *op. cit.* p. 347.
7 Jane Austen, *Sense and Sensibility*, ch. XVIII.
8 *Ibid.* ch. XVIII.
9 This argument is from John Jones, *On Aristotle and Greek Tragedy* (London, 1968), pp. 85-8. The quoted sentences occur on p. 86.
10 Norman N. Holland, *The Dynamics of Literary Response* (New York, 1968), pp. 110-11.
11 *Ibid.* pp. 106-7.
12 Second-order judgments are typically generalisations concerning groups of works or assertions about the relationship of the work to its time, its author, and its audience, and occur in literary history, discussion of literary kinds, biography etc.:

> The idea of a conflict from which there is no escape has become the pivot of modern theories (of tragedy) and has been called the essential condition of a tragic situation. But this leads to difficulties. There can be no doubt that the *Oresteia* of Aeschylus is one of the greatest of Greek dramas. But the ending of this tremendous poem does not leave man broken by the insoluble conflicts which have emerged in the play; it embodies a reconciliation so far-reaching that it embraces the world of the gods as well as man in his suffering (Albin Lesky, *Greek Tragedy*, trans. H A Frankfort (London, 1965), pp. 11-12).

Here Goethe's requirement that tragedy should embody 'the idea of a conflict from which there is no escape', is attacked by pointing to the *Oresteia* and giving a description of its ending which is the outcome of an appreciation of the trilogy. A different interpretation of it would, perhaps, support Goethe's second-order judgments. Second-order judgments are of limited interest in the present discussion where the important distinction is between appreciation and judgments of mere understanding.

IV

FICTION AND REALITY

Peter Lamarque

And as imagination bodies forth
The forms of things unknown, the poet's pen
Turns them into shapes, and gives to airy nothing
A local habitation and a name.
(*A Midsummer Night's Dream* V, i, 14–17)

I

There is a logical puzzle at the heart of the theory of literature. It concerns fictional characters. The puzzle is simply this: What exactly *are* fictional characters? We talk readily and authoritatively of Faustus and Fanny Price, Tom Sawyer and Uncle Toby, and often delight in doing so. Furthermore, we acquire beliefs about them and even argue about their true nature. Yet there are no such people and we know that perfectly well. Is all this talk, then, about *nothing at all?* What is fictional, to be sure, cannot be *real* but characters it seems cannot be *nothing*. So what in the world are we talking about? That is the puzzle I want to explore.

The logical issue here revolves round problems of reference and existence. It is distinct from other issues that arise about the relations between fiction and reality. We often ask what items or aspects of reality a fictional character is *based* on, what if anything it *coincides* with or is *true* to or what *gave rise* to it. But these questions about causal or accidental relations presuppose the more fundamental, logical questions concerning what fictions are and what relations *can* obtain between them and the real world.[1]

To say without qualification that fictional characters do not exist only compounds the mystery of how it is we can acquire true or false beliefs about them and how we can become so intimate with them. To say that they exist-in-fiction is not to explain anything; for it is true only inasmuch as it repeats again that they are fictional. A more promising start is to notice, following Nelson Goodman, that while unicorns do not exist, unicorn-pictures and unicorn-descriptions do exist.[2] Similarly, though Faustus does not exist, Faustus-characterisations certainly do; and we know where to find them. Our investigation of fictions and fictional creatures must begin with these descriptions and characterisations. The logical problems of fictional reference and existence have their origins in the peculiarities of fictional narratives and stories.

II

In virtue of what is a story or narrative *fictional* or a *work of fiction*? We will look in vain, I believe, for formal or intrinsic properties of discourse which serve to identify a narrative conclusively as fictional. There seem to be two classes of such properties which are promising candidates: let us call them *surface* and *semantic* properties.

Surface properties would include, for example, syntactic and stylistic constructions. However, from a logical point of view, fictional writing cannot be conclusively identified as distinct from historical or non-fictional writing, solely by reference to its surface features. This is not to deny of course that there are characteristic surface features of fictional writing; David Lodge, in *The Modes of Modern Writing*, has identified such features with some illuminating comparisons of fictional and journalistic descriptions of execution by hanging. It is only to say that these characteristic features are not strictly necessary or sufficient for the writing to be fictional. After all, historical narrative can appear in many guises.

Semantic properties are those relating to reference and truth. Again, there are characteristic semantic features of fictional writing: the proper names have no objects of reference in the real world and the descriptions are not true of anything in the real world. But again, perhaps surprisingly, these characteristic features in themselves seem to be neither necessary nor sufficient: not necessary, because it might just be that things in the world do fit the descriptions and names, not sufficient because non-fictional historical writing might just fail in its own references and descriptions.

What we must conclude is that the property 'being a work of fiction' is not reducible to any set of surface or semantic properties of language but it is at least partly, and essentially, to do with *intention* and *use*. Roughly speaking we can say this, contrasting fiction with history. A historical work (including biography or autobiography) is produced with the intention of describing, explaining or reconstructing past, and actual, events. It is written for the most part in an assertoric mode and invites assessment by such criteria as accuracy, truth and consistency with known fact. It is subject to verification and refutation. A fictional work, on the other hand, is produced with the intention of presenting and describing imaginary people and events. It is not written in an assertoric mode and does not invite assessment under the canons of assertion and factual truth. It is not subject to verification and refutation. Characterised in this way, the difference between historical and fictional writing resides essentially in the different *purposes* for which each is produced and the different *commitments* that arise from these purposes. The conventions of story-telling release us from the commitment of truth-telling and belief without incurring any blame or censure. The lack of intended deceit distinguishes writing a fiction and telling a lie.

Let me forestall a possible confusion. I have been speaking of fiction *per se* and although that includes all literary fiction it is not so clear that it includes all literature. Not all fiction is literature, certainly, and perhaps not all literature is fiction. We sometimes apply the term 'literature' to writing that was intended to take on the commitments of ordinary descriptive discourse: Gibbon's *Decline and Fall*, for example, or Boswell's *Life of Johnson*, maybe even the Bible. It has been suggested that to read discourse as literature is *ipso facto* to read it *as fiction*.[3] But even if this is right it does not serve to identify literature with fiction. For the attitude that a reader takes to a work need not coincide with that of the writer and it is the writer's intentions that determine fictionality. John Searle has summarised the point succinctly: 'Whether or not a work is literature is for the readers to decide, whether or not it is fictional is for the author to decide.'[4]

Identifying fiction in terms of the intentions and purposes of a writer of fiction might not in itself take us very far towards explaining the logical connection between fiction and reality. But locating fiction within the framework of a theory of language use, rather than with reference to syntactic or semantic properties, has far-reaching consequences for most of the central problems surrounding the logic of fiction. For, most important of all, it provides an appropriate context for explaining the special referential function of names in fiction. And that in turn will yield explanations of what kinds of things fictional characters are and how we can talk or hold beliefs about them.

III

Consider the following, not untypical, passage from Fielding's *Tom Jones*:

> It was now the middle of May, and the morning was remarkably serene, when Mr Allworthy walked forth on the terrace, where the dawn opened every minute that lovely prospect we have before described to his eye. And now, having sent forth streams of light, which ascended the blue firmament before him as harbingers preceding his pomp, in the full blaze of his majesty rose the sun; than which one object alone in this lower creation could be more glorious, and that Mr Allworthy himself presented: a human being replete with benevolence, meditating in what manner he might render himself most acceptable to his Creator by doing most good to his creatures.
>
> Reader, take care; I have unadvisedly led thee to the top of as high a hill as Mr Allworthy's, and how to get thee down without breaking my neck I do not well know. However, let us e'en venture to slide down together, for Miss Bridget rings her bell and Mr Allworthy is summoned to breakfast, where I must attend, and, if you please, should be glad of your company (Book I, chapter 4).

For all its ironic and metaphorical nature, there is nothing intrinsic to this passage that determines it must be fictional. Indeed, the presence of the personal pronouns 'I' and 'thee' if anything increases the surface appearance of its not being fictional. But fictional it is; the sentences come from a novel, the characters are inventions of Fielding's.

Let us now pursue in more detail the general suggestion made earlier that the defining properties of fictional narrative are to be found in intention and use. It is helpful to distinguish the *propositional content* or sense of a sentence from the *illocutionary intentions* or force with which it is presented.

According to the use theory of fiction, what makes sentences fictional are the illocutionary intentions behind their utterance, not their sense. An illocutionary intention is an intention to perform an 'illocutionary act', for example, that of asserting, questioning, promising or warning. There are rules governing the correct performance of such illocutionary acts: thus, to assert is to take on a commitment to the truth of what is asserted, a sincere assertion requires the speaker's belief in what is asserted, and so on. In fiction, the story-teller gives the appearance of performing illocutionary acts but, due to the conventions of story-telling, he in fact takes on none of the commitments associated with these illocutionary acts; the rules are suspended, the normal illocutionary intentions are missing. R M Gale has described this as 'illocutionary disengagement'.[5] In the passage from *Tom Jones*, Fielding gives the appearance of performing illocutionary acts: for example, *stating* ('. . . the morning was remarkably serene'), *warning* ('Reader, take care'), and *inviting* ('I . . . should be glad of your company'). But the corresponding commitments are lacking: in reality there is no such morning in the middle of May, the reader is in no danger, and there is no real breakfast that the reader could attend.

John Searle and others have suggested that in fiction a writer *pretends* to perform illocutionary acts, though without any intended deception.[6] While I think in general this is a useful description of what a fiction writer is doing, nevertheless it can be misleading. For one thing, what pretence there is covers only the force of the utterances, not their sense or content. A writer is not pretending to express propositions, only pretending to assert them as true.

Also, and this is a point often overlooked in pretence theories, not all illocutionary intentions in fiction are pretended. Take the warning in the passage quoted. The reader is apparently being warned against breaking his neck while descending a hill on Mr Allworthy's estate. Taken literally, no such warning could be heeded. But there are clear indications that the hill is to be taken metaphorically; the heights are of a prose-style, not a landscape. We are being warned against taking too seriously the exaggerated description of Mr Allworthy in the preceding paragraph. Fielding even spells this out for us in his chapter heading: 'The reader's neck brought into danger by a description.' There is, then, a genuine warning here, and one that could and should be heeded. But recognition of the commitments underlying the genuine warning is only triggered by recognition that the commitments of the apparent illocutionary intentions have been suspended. Similar remarks could be made about the invitation. We cannot, indeed, join Mr Allworthy over breakfast. But, for all that, there is a genuine invitation here, namely, to get involved with the characters, to develop an intimacy with them, to think of them as our companions, and so on. Although illocutionary intentions are not always what they seem in fiction, and standard commitments are suspended, there are genuine illocutionary intentions which we as readers must recognise.[7] Fielding, in this passage, is *parodying* a flowery prose-style, *deflating* pompous sentiments, *warning* readers not to take everything they read too seriously, and *inviting* them to relax and feel comfortable with the characters.

The propositional content or sense of a sentence is that part which stays constant through changes of illocutionary force in the utterance of the sentence. We can state that the door is shut, we can ask whether it is shut, we can order that it be shut and we can promise to shut it. We can think of all such contexts as possessing a common propositional content, *that the door is shut*, which could be made explicit by suitable paraphrase of the force indicating verbs. Sentences in fictional stories also possess a propositional content and this content is just what it would be if the sentences appeared in other, non-fictional contexts. This is only to say that we could understand the sentences without knowing whether they are true or false. To understand them we need only know under what conditions they would be true if asserted. This point is of some consequence for the issue of the connection between fiction and reality. Before enlarging on it, and giving a closer characterisation of propositional content, I fear it is necessary to take another detour and introduce another set of distinctions.

IV

Consider the sentence:

(1) Miss Bridget rings her bell and Mr Allworthy is summoned to breakfast.

There are at least three contexts in which this sentence might be used. First, there is the context where it has indeed been used, namely, by Fielding in *Tom Jones*. Let us call this *the author's use*. Then there is the use by a person describing what occurs in the story, knowing that it is part of a story. Let us call this *an informed reader's use*. Finally, we can think of this sentence being used by someone who, on reading the story, believes that Miss Bridget and Mr Allworthy are real people and that these events have actually taken place. Let us call this *a misinformed reader's use*. Now these uses are distinct.

The author's use is not an assertion; it occurs within the activity of telling a story and as such the rules of assertion are suspended. It is, perhaps, at most a pretended assertion. Likewise, the apparent references by means of the proper names are not real references, they too are pretended references or, more precisely, as we shall see, they are pretended references to *people*. Here we can see the difference between history and fiction at its most stark. The historian makes assertions and thereby describes, truly or falsely, independently existing states of affairs. A writer of fiction, in an author's use of a sentence, makes no assertion and in using the sentence *stipulates* fictional states of affairs. There is no question of correspondence with the facts and thus no truth-value can be appropriately assigned to a sentence in an author's use.

An informed reader's use is different from an author's use, even when the same sentence is involved. An informed reader, knowingly talking of a fiction, can use the sentence (1) to make an assertion, assessable as true or false. Of course a reader could be merely quoting or reading the sentence, or using it to *retell* (part of) the story, in which case, as with an author's use, no assertion would be intended.[8] But where an assertion is intended, it is *about the story*. In such a use, (1) can be thought of as elliptical for some such sentence as 'In Fielding's *Tom Jones*, Miss Bridget rings her bell . . . '. In this case the assertion would be true and its truth derives directly from the author's use of (1). The references are not pretended references but real references to components of the story, that is, to characters (what that means we will come to later). Here there are some similarities between history and fiction. The reader of fiction, like the reader of history, acquires beliefs, true or false; the former acquires beliefs about *what occurs in the story*, while the latter acquires beliefs about *what occurs in the world*. These beliefs can be the basis for true or false assertions, be they about a story or about the world. Further, the acquisition of beliefs in both cases can call for investigation, the collection of evidence and the assessment of data. In the case of fiction, readers are called upon to *supplement* what appears explicitly in the sentences of the fiction, usually by reference to assumed shared background knowledge,[9] and even to *reject* or *modify* what appears explicitly. Is Mr Allworthy truly 'a human being replete with benevolence'? From this passage alone it would be rash to draw such a conclusion; after all, the reader is warned to 'take care'. The nature of Mr Allworthy has to be constructed from all the information supplied, carefully filtered through the layers of irony, hyperbole and fictional speaker's prejudice.

Finally, there is the misinformed reader's use, made under the mistaken belief that the proper names refer to real people. Here, unlike the informed reader's use, there is no implicit fictional operator. We can say that an *attempted* assertion is made, about actual events, but because of a radical failure of reference in this use of the proper names the assertion is defective. Nothing true or false has been said about real people because there are no real people involved. Of our three uses only the misinformed reader's use can be described as a reference failure.

V

We can now return to the question of the propositional content of sentences in, and about, fiction. Here it is instructive to recall certain suggestions made by Frege. According to Frege, when we read fiction, or indeed poetry, our interest is concentrated on the *thoughts* or propositions expressed rather than on the *reference* or *truth-value* of what is expressed.

> In hearing an epic poem, . . . apart from the euphony of the language we are interested only in the sense of the sentences and the images and feelings thereby aroused. The question of truth would cause us to abandon aesthetic delight for an attitude of scientific investigation.[10]

This re-direction of our attention from reference to sense is one consequence of the fact, in our own terms, that the sense of a sentence, in an author's use, is not asserted and the apparent references are merely pretended.

Those sentences in fiction which do not contain names of fictional characters, for example, sentences of the kind 'The morning was remarkably serene', present no special problem when it comes to identifying propositional content. The content or sense of such sentences in either an author's use or an informed reader's use is just what it is in non-fictional uses, as determined by conventional truth-conditions. The sense is not affected by the fictional context. All that happens is that in the author's use the fictional or story-telling context suspends the normal conditions governing an assertive force of the sentence. In an informed reader's use, the assertive force is again suspended from the sentence itself, though it reappears governing the wider, more explicit sentence with the prefix 'In the novel . . . '. This wider sentence, as we have seen, can be used to make an assertion about the novel. In effect it says that the novel expresses (or implies) the sense of the component sentence.

Identifying the propositional content of sentences in fiction which contain the names of fictional characters is a little more complex. But the principles are the same. Again the distinction is needed between the sense of the sentences and the standard illocutionary force or intentions with which they are used. How do these proper names operate in sentences in fiction? Although, in sentences like (1), they have the appearance of being ordinary names of people, and as such might take in the misinformed reader, this is of course not the referential function they have in either the author's use or an informed reader's use. The standard referential intentions associated with such names are suspended. For in these uses the names refer not to people but to fictional characters. But what does that mean? Here we must tread carefully.

The danger in talk about fictional characters is to confuse what might be called an *internal perspective*, from within stories, with an *external perspective*, from the real world. Within stories, fictional characters are indeed ordinary people, at least those of the Miss Bridget and Mr Allworthy kind. Furthermore, within the story of *Tom Jones*, Mr Allworthy can refer to Miss Bridget, and say true or false things about her, just as he can have breakfast with her. Within the story, that is, from an internal perspective, the names 'Miss Bridget' and 'Mr Allworthy' function as ordinary proper names referring to ordinary people. Let us call this an *internal* use. Now an internal use is only possible for a speaker within a story. The appearance of these same names in an author's or informed reader's use, say, of sentence (1) must fall under an external perspective. This will be an *external* use. To understand what it means to *refer to a fictional character* we must explore the logic of such external use.

It is to Frege again that we owe the insight that in certain contexts names lose what he called their 'customary reference' and take on an 'indirect reference' which he identified as their 'customary sense'. These contexts, according to Frege, including, for example, reports of people's beliefs, bring about a shift from reference to sense. A name appearing in such a context comes to refer only to its sense rather than to the object of its customary reference. Now both an author's use and an informed reader's use of sentences containing names of fictional characters can be thought of as just such contexts. The clue here is to observe certain similarities between sentences under the scope of prefixes like 'A believes that . . . ' and sentences following the prefix, 'In such-and-such a novel . . . '. Both contexts, for example, block existential generalisation. From 'John believes that he saw the Loch Ness monster' we cannot infer that the Loch Ness monster exists, just as we cannot infer that Mr Allworthy exists from the true claim that 'In the novel, Mr Allworthy is summoned to breakfast'. Now pursuing the parallel with names in belief-contexts we can think of the internal reference of names of fictional characters as something like their customary reference and the external reference of such names as their indirect reference. My suggestion then is this. When names of fictional characters appear in the context of either an author's use or an informed reader's use, that is, when they are used from an external perspective, *the internal references of the names, i.e. to the ordinary people in the story, get transformed into indirect references, i.e. to the senses of the names themselves.* In short, proper names of fictional characters, as used by an author or an informed reader, refer only to senses, not to persons or particulars of any kind. The names lose the internal references they have when used by other fictional characters. What that means is that we, of course, cannot refer to fictional characters in the way that other characters can. From our perspective, *we* can refer only to the *senses* of the names *they* use to refer to *persons.*

What is the sense of a proper name? Since Mill pronounced that proper names have denotation but no connotation, the question of whether proper names can be said to possess a sense has been a matter of perennial philosophical controversy. I cannot debate the issue here but will simply propose that names at least of fictional characters should be thought of as having a sense. I do not see this as committing me to the view that all names have senses. I take the sense of a name, where there is one, to be, roughly, what Frege called the 'mode of presentation' of the reference of the name or, as characterised by Michael Dummett, *the means by which a name identifies its reference.* In connection with the names of fictional characters the reference here will of course be internal reference, that is, the reference to persons within stories. The sense of a fictional name is the means by which a fictional person is presented and identified in a story. It can be specified by descriptions and predicates which serve to identify the internal reference. So, for example, the sense of the name 'Mr Allworthy' will be given by those descriptions in, or derivable from, the novel *Tom Jones* which identify the fictional Mr Allworthy: the person called 'Mr Allworthy', who found the infant Tom Jones lying in his bed, who banished him from his home after being deceived by Master Blifil, who in the end reached a warm-hearted reconciliation, and so on. These descriptions can be said both to *identify the person* Mr Allworthy, from the internal perspective, and *define the character* Mr Allworthy, from the external perspective. They give the sense of the name which becomes the object of reference in an external use. This sense identifies for us a set of properties which constitutes a fictional character. And finally it is this sense that becomes a constituent of the propositional content of sentences in which the name appears in either an author's or an informed reader's use.

VI

The theoretical framework outlined here offers some immediate benefits towards explaining many of the remaining puzzles concerning the relations between fiction and reality. First of all, we can now explain our intuition about fictional characters that as fictions they cannot be real but as characters they cannot be nothing. Fictional characters, like Mr Allworthy or Miss Bridget, do not exist in the real world *as persons*. They are fictional-persons or persons-in-a-story, to be contrasted perhaps with fictional-robots or fictional-elephants, but that of course does not entail that they are in fact persons. As characters, though, they can be said to exist, but only as *abstract* entities, that is, as concepts or sets of properties.[11] What in a fictional world are persons are merely characters or abstract entities in the real world. The Fregean shift from internal to external reference is precisely the shift from internal reference to persons to external reference to characters. The persons do not exist but the characters do.[12]

Identifying characters as abstract entities from the external perspective accords with the etymology of the word 'character'. The word belongs with other abstract nouns like 'characterisation' or 'personality'. There is even a conventional device in English for referring to the *character* of an actual person without referring to the *person* as an individual. We speak of so-and-so being a *Napolean* or an *Einstein* or of someone's being the *Genghis Khan* of the philosophy department or *the Nixon* of the Reagan Administration. This is a rhetorically powerful way of identifying and ascribing properties, namely those commonly attributed to the person whose name is used. Furthermore, it is easy enough, story-telling apart, to describe a character not exemplified by, or drawn from, any (one) actual person; a criminologist or psychologist, for example, might do so in constructing a 'profile' or 'type'. A novelist in describing a character does much the same as these, though probably in more detail and no doubt for different ends. The labelling of a fictional personality or character with a proper name is of no logical significance and does not affect its abstract nature. It simply aids the effectiveness of the story-teller's pretence.

It might be objected that a novelist, in presenting a 'rounded' character, is not presenting a *type*, as a psychologist or criminologist might be, but rather something unique and individual. But the claim that fictional characters are individuals, at least from the external perspective, is simply false; it involves a category mistake. What we correctly call the uniqueness, even individuality, of some fictional characters is entirely a feature of the combination and perhaps complexity of the properties that constitute them. Even if, by coincidence, all the properties comprising a fictional character were found to be instantiated in one individual in the real world, it would still be wrong to identify that individual with that character. No individual can be a character, again precisely because a character belongs essentially in the category of abstract entities.

Another advantage of the theory is that it explains how it is that readers have no difficulty understanding fictional stories, at least with respect to their being fictional. Once the convention of pretence in story-telling has been grasped, which allows for the suspension of normal illocutionary (and referential) intentions, and the focus of interest turns to the senses or propositional contents of the story's sentences, there is no further barrier to understanding. Grasping the senses of sentences in fictions is no different from grasping the senses of non-fictional sentences. We can think of an author, following the conventions of story-telling, as *presenting* (but not asserting, etc.) *propositions for our consideration*.[13]

When we reflect on the senses of these propositions, including the descriptive senses of the fictional proper names, we are reflecting on concepts and properties which are likely in themselves to be familiar to us through exemplification in the real world. Although we would not expect to find in the world exactly the combination of properties which constitute the character of Mr Allworthy, nevertheless we will recognize in people of our acquaintance many of the constitutive properties or significant combinations of them. We can take up Fielding's invitation to *get to know* the characters better by using our imagination to call to mind their constitutive properties as we entertain, and reflect on, the descriptions and propositions presented by the author. As we have seen, we also need to supplement the author's descriptions by pursuing certain of their implications against an assumed background. We draw on what we know about actual people, those for example similar in significant respects, in order to 'round out' the characters with supplementary properties. Here disputes between readers are likely to be at their most acute. All in all, this imaginative exercise goes a long way, I think, towards explaining the pleasure or even instruction associated with fictional works of literature.

Of course, corresponding to the imaginative exercise of readers in understanding a fiction is the imaginative effort of writers in creating a fiction. Our theory accords well with the practice of writing fiction in stressing the idea of the construction of characters by formulating descriptions which identify properties. From a logical point of view, a writer is free to draw on any properties he pleases in constructing a character, though of course in practice there will be constraints of plausibility, verisimilitude and aesthetic coherence.

The theory has the further benefit of providing a straightforward explanation for the notorious problem of the 'incompleteness' of fictional characters. Characters are radically unlike individuals in that for a great number of properties it seems to be neither true that they have that property nor true that they do not have that property: hence the much discussed case of the mole on Sherlock Holmes' back.[14] There is nothing in the Holmes canon that indicates whether Holmes does or does not have a mole on his back and there is no form of inference that will allow us to determine the matter one way or the other. Accounts of fictional characters as possible individuals will have difficulty accommodating facts such as this; individuals, it seems, must either possess or lack every property. But if characters are no more than sets of properties then there is no requirement that every property or its negation be a member of the set. The set, after all, is made up of just those properties designated or implied by the author. Of course even though the constitutive set does not contain property P or property not-P that is not to say that it might not contain the disjunctive property *either P or not-P*. Sherlock Holmes, being a fictional person, and not a logical freak, no doubt possesses the disjunctive property of either having a mole on his back or not;[15] but it does not follow that the property of having a mole is in the Holmes-constitutive set or the property of not having a mole is in the set.[16]

Another advantage of the theory is that it accounts for how fiction can be realistic. A fiction is realistic if it describes characters with combinations of properties that would not be strange or out of place if exemplified in individuals in the real world. More interestingly, it affords an explanation of our response to certain forms of allegorical, fantasy or science fiction writing. How is it, for example, that a novel like Orwell's *Animal Farm* can strike us as 'realistic' or 'true to life' when ostensibly it describes a world radically different from our own, one in which farmyard animals speak, think and reason exactly like human beings? Many children's stories present the same problem. An account of fiction in terms of possible worlds would require us to conceive the world of *Animal Farm* as radically different from our own world. Yet this runs counter to our intuition that the power of the novel resides precisely in its striking similarity to the real world. Of course, what is needed here is an appeal to levels of interpretation or understanding. On one level, we say, the story is about farmyard animals, on another, easily recognisable level it is about people and political ideologies. Our theory of fictional characters can help to explicate the metaphor of 'levels' here. For we can think of these as different stages in the abstraction of properties. On the literal, and surface, level the characters are identified with all the properties attributed directly, or implicitly, to them in the novel. At another level, we can abstract and then set aside those properties which belong specifically to farmyard animals, being left as a result with only those properties attributable to familiar humans. It is these remaining properties, forming of course a major component of the characters, which come to the fore when we react to the book as being 'true to life'. The ease with which we can move between these different levels is straightforwardly explicable on the view that fictional characters are sets of properties. For what is happening is that we direct our attention to particular members or subsets of a total set of constituent properties; and that presents no special imaginative or intellectual difficulty. It is just this possibility of selective attention that explains how we can recognise ordinary human qualities in the most bizarre or outrageous fictional creatures.

Finally, the theory can be used to explain the possibility of emotional response to fictional characters. The emotions can be seen as directed to mental representations characterised by just those descriptions that identify the characters and fictional events. I will not develop this account here as I have done so elsewhere[17] and this vexed and difficult topic deserves treatment in its own right.

VII

I will now raise, and attempt to answer, certain difficulties that seem to arise for the theory and in doing so will offer further refinements of it.[18] A logical account of the relation of fiction to reality must explain how we can say true or false things about fictional characters. The complication is that there seem to be different kinds of things we can say, truly or falsely, about characters; there are different kinds of predication.[19] Consider, for example, the following:

(A1) Fielding created Mr Allworthy
(A2) Mr Allworthy is a fictional character
(B3) Mr Allworthy grew fond of Tom Jones
(B4) Mr Allworthy is an honest and forgiving man
(C5) Tom Jones would have been a hippy in the 1960s
(C6) Tom Jones would never have married Fanny Price

The sentences (A1) and (A2) contain the fictional name 'Mr Allworthy' but do not seem to be amenable to analysis in terms of either an author's use or an informed reader's use. That is, the sentences are not presented as part of a story with standard illocutionary forces suspended yet nor do they seem to be paraphrasable into sentences containing the intensional operator, 'In the fiction (novel) . . . '. Both, however, seem to be true and able to be asserted. I think the best way to understand the use of the name 'Mr Allworthy' in such sentences is as a truncated form of the description, 'the Mr Allworthy-character'. This use is made possible by prior occurrences of the name in an author's use. Here the reference to the character is direct and explicit. However, the original Fregean analysis can still be applied. For we can think of the context, 'the _____-character' as an intensional context in which a name has only its indirect reference. In definite descriptions of the kind, 'the X-character', the character is identified through the sense of the name.

To say that the Mr Allworthy-character is fictional, as in (A2), is to say that the name, and constituent properties, are introduced in a fiction under the conventions of story-telling. It is not to say that there is no individual in the world which possesses the properties, even though that is probably the case. To say that Mr Allworthy *does not exist*, is I think ambiguous between saying that the character is fictional, a claim about its presentation, and saying that no individual realises the constituent properties, a claim about its instantiation. The truth-conditions under these two readings are different.

There is a further problem about sentence (A1). Strictly speaking, if a character is a set of properties, a writer cannot truly be said to *create* a character. Fielding did not create the properties constituent of Mr Allworthy so correspondingly he did not create the set of those properties. It might be thought a weakness of the theory that it should have such a seemingly paradoxical consequence. However, I think that everything we want from sentence (A1), in so far as it expresses a truth, can be captured in some, albeit prosaic, paraphrase of the form: 'Fielding presented for our attention through his creative choice of descriptions the Mr Allworthy-character.' Fielding's, and any author's, creativity and imaginative skill reside in the careful use of descriptive language to identify and juxtapose complex combinations of properties.

The (B)-sentences offer a different kind of predication from the (A)-sentences.[20] We have seen how sentences of the (B) kind can be analysed in an author's or informed reader's use such that the name 'Mr Allworthy' comes to make an indirect reference to the sense of the name. This sense, and thus new reference, can be thought of as identifying a set of properties as determined by descriptions elsewhere in the fiction. It would be a mistake, though, to suppose that the predicates 'grew fond of Tom Jones' and 'is an honest and forgiving man' are being applied in (B3) and (B4) directly to *sets of properties*. This would make the sentences categorially absurd. (B4) does not assert that a *set* is honest and forgiving. What we must say, strictly speaking, is that the predicates are not so much *true of* the character (though from an internal perspective they are true of a person within the novel) but rather identify properties that are *included in* the set of properties that constitutes the character. In an author's use this membership is being *stipulated*, in a reader's use it is being *reported*.

Sentence (B3) suggests a difficulty for the identification of characters. A full specification of the constituent properties of Mr Allworthy will require reference to Tom Jones, and other characters, but likewise a full specification of the constituent properties of Tom Jones will require reference to Mr Allworthy. Does this involve a vicious circularity? I think not. If the problem is one of assigning a truth-value to sentences like (B3) in an informed reader's use then we can do so simply on the basis of an identifying core of non-relational properties associated with each character. If the problem is one of the independent identity of characters then we should recall that the distinctness of characters one from another is determined entirely by the distinctness of whole sets of constitutive properties. Relations between characters will not jeopardise their mutual independence in this sense.

The third category of predications concerns counterfactual attributions: in the case of (C5), concerning a fictional character *vis-à-vis* the real world, in the case of (C6), concerning characters from different fictions. Although we might have difficulty assigning a definite truth-value in such examples, we do at least feel that the sentences make sense. What, then, are their truth-conditions? We should remember that it is only from the perspective of the real world that characters are sets of properties; from the internal perspective of the story they are persons. So from the perspective of some possible world other than the real world we can also think of them as persons, exemplifying in that world those properties which identify a person in the original fiction and constitute a character in the real world. Roughly speaking, the truth-conditions of (C5) rest on the relation between the Tom

Jones characteristics as described in *Tom Jones* and the hippy characteristics as perceived in the 1960s. More specifically, I suggest that we are being asked to conceive of a world in which the maximum number of (important) properties of the Tom Jones character are realised in some individual and which also conforms to the background of the 1960s and compare it with other similar worlds in which a comparable individual does or does not possess the properties associated with being a hippy. What is important is not what result would be obtained from this investigation but rather the underlying principle of counterfactual reasoning about characters. This principle, which involves the maximal realisation of properties in individuals across worlds (other than the real world where the character is simply an abstract entity), applies as well to cases such as (C6). In this example, again under an informal characterisation, we must consider worlds where the Tom Jones set of properties is maximally realised in some individual and the Fanny Price set is maximally realised and then ask of these worlds whether it is those in which the individuals get married or those in which they do not that preserve the best balance between an assumed background and the (important) properties of the two characters. The rationale for this account is that if we want to enquire what fictional characters would be like under different conditions our speculations can best proceed by conceiving the exemplification of the characters in individuals in different worlds. In effect we are comparing alternative fictions preserving as much as possible of the original.

My appeal to the modal logician's notion of possible worlds is strictly limited to explaining a certain type of reasoning about fictional characters. The view I have developed overall, which sees characters as abstract entities in the real world, is distinct from those views which see them only as individuals in possible worlds. One merit, as I see it, of the account here is that it allows in principle for characters to possess logically incompatible or contradictory properties. If a character is constituted by a set of properties there is no reason why that set should not contain contradictory properties identified perhaps explicitly by predicates F and not-F in a fictional narrative. There might not be much aesthetic merit in such a character but a theory of fiction should be able to accommodate the total freedom of a writer to stipulate whatever properties he likes for a fictional construct. Writers are not confined to describing possible worlds. Of course, no character which does have contradictory properties could be the subject of counterfactual reasoning which involves the realisation of the character in individuals across worlds, at least not until the contradiction has been eliminated in some way. Also, no such character, with the contradiction intact, could be pictured or imagined by readers.

If a fictional character is constituted by a set of properties, then any change in the membership of the set will produce a different character. A character possesses its constituent properties essentially. It might seem that this inflexibility produces undesirable consequences for the theory. For example, don't our intuitions suggest that Tom Jones *might have been different*? Was it *necessary* that he did everything just so? Here, though, we are trading on a recurrent ambivalence about characters, arising from their likeness to real persons. What might have been different is not Tom Jones but *Tom Jones*. Fielding might have written a different novel under the title 'Tom Jones'. In this different novel a central character named 'Tom Jones' might have been portrayed with properties different from those possessed by Tom Jones. But this alternative Tom Jones would, strictly speaking, be a different character from the one that we have, however similar their constituent properties. A character is what it is stipulated to be by an author, though an author might have stipulated differently.

It might be objected to this reply that it discounts the possibility that the same character might appear in different novels, being ascribed different properties. Three kinds of case come to mind here. Certain characters, like Sherlock Holmes, Plantagenet Palliser and George Smiley, appear in a series of stories. Is it the same character in each member of the series? Surely it is. Here we can think of each series as comprising a single fiction. The properties that constitute the characters are those ascribed to them in all the novels in the series; until the series is complete the character itself, strictly speaking, is not complete, though we might possess a great deal of information about it. A second case concerns a novel that is re-written. John Fowles, for example, has produced a second, and altered version of *The Magus*. Do the same characters appear in the re-written novel? I think that the correct answer here is similar to the answer to the third kind of case. These are cases in which a writer takes over, as we might say, characters from the fictions of other writers and, in a new story, or a new version of an old story, gives them different and even incompatible properties. Faust, for example, is described by Goethe and Marlowe, Rosencrantz by Shakespeare and Tom Stoppard. Is it the same character in the different stories? I think the best approach here, following a suggestion by Nicholas Wolterstorff, is to distinguish, as he describes it, the Faust character *simpliciter* from the Faust-in-Goethe's-*Faust*-character and the Faustus-in-Marlowe's *Dr Faustus*-character.[21] The set of properties constituting the Faust-character *simpliciter* consists only of certain core properties, essential to something's earning the title 'Faust' in any version. The Goethe and Marlowe characters contain this core, and as such qualify for the name 'Faust', but also contain more properties as well. With respect to the core they are the same, with respect to the further characterisations they are different. I suggest then that normally what we mean by saying that the same character appears in different fictions, including the characters in the two versions of *The Magus*, is that the same significant *core* of properties is identified as constitutive of some (fictional) individual in the different stories. Where our concern is with fine details beyond this core, and where these differ, we must say in that respect that the characters too are different.

In practice, of course, appeal to a core of properties is important to explain our epistemic relations with fictional characters. For with respect to complex characters we rarely know, and indeed are rarely interested in, all the properties that constitute a character. This, however, leads to a difficulty given our association of the sets of properties constituting a character and the sense of fictional names. For if we do not know all the properties that constitute a character can we truly be said to understand sentences containing the name of that character? There are two distinct issues here. The first concerns what it is to *know* or *identify* a character, the second what it is to understand sentences about characters.

It would seem that to know a character is to know what properties belong in the set constitutive of that character. But, as I say, complete knowledge of that kind is rare. We need some notion of the *partial* knowledge of a character, or knowledge *sufficient for identification*. There seem to be at least two components of such partial knowledge. One is the requirement that we know some central core of properties belonging to the character-set; the other is that we are able to give a general characterisation of the set itself, for example through specifying a *route* by which the remaining members could be identified. So *partial* knowledge of Tom Jones (that is, sufficient for identification) requires not only a knowledge of salient properties comprising the character but also knowledge that this is a character whose constitutive properties can be discovered in a certain way, e.g. directly through reading Fielding's novel or indirectly through summaries or descriptions of the novel. We do not have adequate knowledge for identifying Tom Jones if we think that he is a real person, even if we do know a large number of his central attributes.

It is partial knowledge of this kind that can be appealed to in answer to our second question concerning what it is to understand sentences about characters. As long as we know a core of properties picked out by a fictional name and some route by which the remaining properties can be identified we have sufficient knowledge to understand a sentence containing the fictional name.

There remains a further and related difficulty, that of accounting for our psychological attitudes to fictional characters. When can we be said to be *thinking about* a particular fictional character?[22] Or liking, admiring, despising or fearing that character? And when can two people be said to be thinking about, admiring, etc. the *same* character? The conditions we have discussed for *identifying* characters or *understanding* sentences containing fictional names are not, I think, sufficient for capturing the appropriate objects of our psychological attitudes towards characters.

Suppose we reflect on the properties: being a kindly squire who brings up a foundling, falls out with him through various misunderstandings but later reaches a happy reconciliation. This reflection is not yet sufficient to qualify as thinking about Fielding's Mr Allworthy even though the content of the reflection captures certain core properties of that character. Not even if one of the properties in our reflection is 'being a man named "Mr Allworthy"' will we have a sufficient condition; indeed that property is not even necessary for reflection on Mr Allworthy. Now suppose that we have the additional belief that the properties in question are attributed to a character in a novel by Fielding. Will that make our original reflection a thought about Fielding's Mr Allworthy? Certainly it establishes a connection between the properties and the novel. But this epistemic connection is not enough, I think, to secure the identification we require of the appropriate psychological attitude. After all, our psychological attitude, in this case reflection or thought but the same goes for admiration, fear and the rest, might have quite the wrong *genesis*. We might have been brought to think about a kindly squire, a foundling, etc. from a source quite independent of Fielding's novel and even though we have certain additional beliefs about that novel and the characters in it, nevertheless, we could not under those conditions be said to be thinking about Mr Allworthy. We might in fact be thinking about some actual person. Our attitudes *to Mr Allworthy* must be anchored to Fielding's novel, not merely epistemically, but *causally*.

Remember that what makes a character *fictional* is precisely that it is presented in a *fiction* by an author under the conventions of story-telling. The author's original use of names and descriptions in a fiction must play some explanatory role in accounting for the attitudes that readers subsequently acquire about the characters so presented. If we are correctly to be said to be thinking about Mr Allworthy there must be a causal route connecting our thoughts with Fielding's use of names and descriptions. As with the epistemic route we discussed earlier, this causal route will either be direct when our reflections or attitudes derive from our reading of the novel or they might be indirect when we come to think about a character not through our own reading of the novel but through someone else's report of it.

In general we can say this: our psychological attitudes towards a fictional character must be anchored through some causal chain to an original *presentation* of that character. This is not surprising when we recall that it is only through an author's use of a fictional name, leading to subsequent uses by informed readers, that references to a character by means of a name are possible. A fictional character is presented by an author in a fiction and that initial presentation must figure in any explanation of subsequent attitudes that readers form towards that character. Suppose, though, that two writers, quite independently, produce two type-identical fictions, perhaps in the manner of Borges' *Pierre Menard*. What can we say about the identity of the characters portrayed? All the internal properties attributed to the characters in the two stories are the same yet they are the products of two separate and independent acts of presentation. I think we must insist that the *same character*, as determined by the constitutive properties, is presented, even though the presentations are distinct in origin. Any subsequent attitudes towards that character will have alternative causal routes back to one or other of the authors. It might even be that the particular presentation with which the attitudes are causally connected makes some difference to the nature of the attitudes themselves. The character-as-presented-by-A and the character-as-presented-by-B, even though the presentations are type-identical, might have different effects on us. Perhaps this is just the point that Borges is making.

Finally, I do not pretend that it is always a straightforward matter determining exactly what properties do constitute any given fictional character. Nor am I certain, in the case of even moderately complex novels, that there is some determinate set of properties associated with each fictional name. As it is, recalling a point emphasised earlier, when reading fiction we are rarely concerned with identifying more than a central core of properties, though a concern with peripheral, as well as central, properties can generate acute critical disagreement. One of the tasks of the literary critic is to weigh the evidence in favour of this property or that. What implications can be drawn from such-and-such a description? How reliable is the testimony of such-and-such a speaker? Beyond this quasi-factual investigation is the further task of *literary interpretation* which involves assigning significance to descriptions within some overall pattern of thematic development. It might be that a character under different interpretations is assigned radically different, even incompatible, properties. If the fiction can support both interpretations we might have to conclude that it projects two different characters under a single proper name. In such cases a character will acquire an identity only *relative to an interpretation*.

VIII

Let me summarise some of the main conclusions and implications of this logical enquiry.

(1)   I hope to have vindicated the common sense view that when critics, or anyone else, talk about fictional characters they are not talking nonsense nor are they speaking, by virtue of their subject-matter, either vacuously, metaphorically or falsely. Their talk can be meaningful, literal and true. It can also be subject to reasoning and based on evidence.

(2)   I have stressed the importance in discussions of 'the language of fiction' of distinguishing *an author's use, an informed reader's use* and *a misinformed reader's use* of sentences and descriptions, even though what is uttered might be the same in each case. Questions of truth and falsity bear differently on these different uses. To speak, as philosophers sometimes do, of fictional names as 'vacuous' or 'empty' or to assimilate them to cases of 'referential failure' is to ignore these important distinctions.

(3)   To characterise an author's use of language in story-telling it is important to distinguish the *identification* of properties through descriptions and propositions and any *assertion* that those properties are instantiated or exemplified in individuals. Only in special circumstances does an author of fiction make assertions.

(4)   To determine what a fictional character is I have drawn on a common sense intuition that a person's *character* is something *abstract* and concerns the person's salient and distinguishing qualities. In general, to speak of a character is to speak of something abstract constituted by properties; we can specify and describe a character whether or not it is exemplified by some real person. A fictional character is a set of properties identified by descriptions under the conventions of story-telling (i.e. in an author's use). This of

course is from an *external* perspective, from our point of view in the real world. From an *internal* perspective, within the world of the fiction, what we call characters exist as ordinary people.

(5) It is sometimes said that when critics discuss fictional characters what they are *really* talking about are either words on a page or ideas in someone's mind. Although neither suggestion corresponds to the view advanced here, the motivating thoughts behind both can be accommodated on this view. A writer will no doubt start with at least a partial idea of a character in his mind identified through reflection on combinations of properties; he will then present and refine the character through descriptions in a story. Creativity and skill reside in both the imaginative and descriptive exercises. It might be that the descriptions themselves help to determine even for the writer what the character is like. In this sense the identity of a fictional character is rooted in the descriptions in a fiction and those descriptions are products of the imagination.

(6) When a reader attributes a property to a fictional character, which strictly speaking is to say that the property is *included* in the constitutive set, he speaks truly only if the property is either identified in relevant descriptions presented by the author or is derivable from those descriptions in suitable ways.

(7) Apart from any *causal* relations between fictional characters and reality, to do with their genesis or their effects, perhaps the most significant relation is something like the traditional *mimesis*. Again on the account given the common sense view is vindicated that fictional characters can be *similar* to real people. The explanation is simple. We will often have observed in real people properties or combinations of properties that we find attributed to characters in a fiction. In this way we *recognise reality* in fiction. We 'see' ourselves and others in fictional characters when we recognise properties identified in fictional descriptions as those exemplified by people we know.

(8) It might be objected that an emphasis on the *abstract* nature of fictional characters is at odds with the *human* interest we take in novels. I think the specificity of 'rounded' characters, as distinct from mere stereotypes, goes a long way towards answering the objection. But also it is worth noting that our interest in humans often itself takes an abstract form. We have a natural curiosity for ideas, attitudes, dilemmas, predicaments, feelings and emotions *in themselves* apart from any particular people who exemplify them. Perhaps this partly explains why our interest in newspaper stories about people unknown to us seems comparable to our interest in fiction. It also explains why fiction can play a serious and instructive part in our lives.

NOTES

1   For a discussion of referential and other relations between fiction and reality, see my 'Bits and Pieces of Fiction', *British Journal of Aesthetics*, forthcoming.

2   Nelson Goodman, 'On Likeness of Meaning', *Analysis*, vol. 10 (1949).

3   Cf. Jonathan Culler, *Structuralist Poetics* (London, 1975), p. 128.

4   J R Searle, 'The Logical Status of Fictional Discourse', *New Literary History*, vol. 6 (1975); reprinted in J R Searle, *Expression and Meaning* (Cambridge, 1979), p. 59.

5   R M Gale, 'The Fictive Use of Language', *Philosophy*, vol. 46 (1971), p. 336.

6   J R Searle, *op. cit.* Related accounts in terms of speech acts can be found in R M Gale, *op. cit.*; Richard Ohmann, 'Speech Acts and the Definition of Literature', *Philosophy and Rhetoric*, vol. 4 (1971); and Monroe Beardsley, 'The Concept of Literature', in F Brady, J Palmer and M Price, *Literary Theory and Structure* (New Haven and London, 1973).

7   A similar point is sometimes made as part of an argument supporting the relevance of authorial intention in literary criticism: e.g. Q Skinner, 'Motives, Intentions and the Interpretations of Texts', *New Literary History*, vol. 3 (1972); and A J Close, '*Don Quixote* and the "Intentionalist Fallacy"', *British Journal of Aesthetics*, vol. 12 (1972).

8   Kendall Walton has suggested that in much of our ordinary discourse about fictional characters we are not making assertions but only *pretending* to do so, in effect continuing the pretence of an author's use (e.g. K Walton, 'How Remote are Fictional Worlds from the Real World?', *Journal of Aesthetics and Art Criticism*, vol. 37 (1978), pp. 20-1). My concern here is with those cases where a speaker offers the sentence *as a truth*.

9   For a useful discussion of the issues involved in making inferences to what is true in fiction, and for further references, see Terence Parsons, *Nonexistent Objects* (New Haven and London, 1980), pp. 175 ff.

10   Gottlob Frege, 'On Sense and Reference', *Philosophical Writings of Gottlob Frege*, translated and edited by P Geach and M Black, 2nd edn (Oxford, 1970), p. 63.

11   For an argument that fictional names are *concept* words, see R Martin and P Schotch, 'The Meaning of Fictional Names', *Philosophical Studies*, vol. 26 (1974); for an argument that characters are *kinds*, see N Wolterstorff, *Works and Worlds of Art* (Oxford, 1980), pt 3:vi. The present paper owes a great deal to these works.

12   See Peter Van Invagen, 'Creatures of Fiction', *American Philosophical Quarterly*, vol. 14 (1977), p. 302, for further reasons for the conclusion that characters exist.

13   I owe this suggestion to A Plantinga, *The Nature of Necessity* (Oxford, 1974), p. 159 and N Wolterstorff, *Works and Worlds of Art* (Oxford, 1980), p. 233.

14   The example is discussed in Wolterstorff, *op. cit.* and Parsons, *op. cit.*

15   If this were not the case, Holmes would be an example of what Howell has called a 'radically incomplete object'. This notion is in contrast to that of a 'nonradically incomplete object' where the matter is simply indeterminate: see R Howell, 'Fictional Objects: How They Are and How They Aren't', *Poetics*, vol. 8 (1979), p. 134; see also Parsons, *op. cit.* pp 183-4.

16   Although I follow the general line of argument here from Parsons *op. cit.* p. 56 and pp. 183-4, and Wolterstorff *op. cit.* p. 147, there is no implication in the present theory that characters are either 'incomplete' (Parsons) or 'non-determinate' (Wolterstorff).

17   See Peter Lamarque, 'How Can We Fear and Pity Fictions?', *British Journal of Aesthetics*, vol. 21 (1981).

18 Here I have benefited considerably from most helpful discussions with Flint Schier and Kit Fine.

19 Howell (*op. cit.*) uses as a test for the adequacy of a theory of fiction how it deals with such different predications.

20 Parsons (*op. cit.* p. 23) marks this difference by distinguishing 'nuclear' predicates (as in (B)) from 'extranuclear' predicates (as in (A)).

21 Wolterstorff, *op. cit.* pp. 148–9.

22 See Lamarque, *op. cit.* pp. 300–1. Various attempts to answer this question are discussed in Howell, *op. cit.*

V

TRAGEDY AND THE COMMUNITY OF SENTIMENT

Flint Schier

I

It is a truth universally acknowledged that fictional characters and their predicaments can have a claim on our sentimental regard. Certainly it cannot be doubted that fictions often stake such a claim. It is equally true that we evaluate our emotional responses to fictions, finding some responses generous, fair and mature while seeing others as miserly, unfair, or sentimental. These two data—for such I take them to be—are obviously two sides of the same coin. A work's claim to an emotional response is justified just when that response is justified.

Simple as this last proposition is, it rules out certain views of when an emotional response to a fiction is legitimate. For example, one might suppose that if a certain emotion would be justified *vis-à-vis* a real situation *p*, then that emotion would be justified *vis-à-vis* a fictive representation of *p*. This is obviously wrong: it might be right for me to pity a homeless orphan, but not every fictive orphan has the right to my pity. Obviously, whether or not a character in a story is entitled to engage our emotional response depends not just upon what happens to him in the story, but on the text's mode of presenting the character and his predicament, upon its style, moral vision and so on. (Nothing hangs here on distinguishing our emotional reactions to the character and our reactions to the story, though I should include the former in the latter but not vice versa.)

By contrast, of course, the style with which an actual event is reported seems to have but little to do with whether a certain emotional reaction to it is appropriate. No matter how feeble and schematic someone's expression of grief or tale of woe, an emotionally generous person will respond to his misery. So we have a *prima facie* distinction between fictive and factive emotion (if I may so label the responses to fiction and fact). The appropriateness of factive emotion depends upon what happened, upon the content of the representation. The appropriateness of fictive emotion depends upon

73

more than the content of the story. One doesn't have to be very wide awake to see that what is at issue here is not so much a distinction between fictive and factive emotions as a distinction between our emotions in an aesthetic context and our emotions in 'real life' contexts. Distinguishing these contexts will depend at least upon pragmatic considerations. For example, if a report of grief has no particular claim upon our interest of the usual sort (it involves no one we know or care about particularly) we will be inclined to make certain 'aesthetic' demands of the story (search for 'aesthetic' motives for telling it to us).

In any case, none but the most frigid aesthete would refuse an emotional response to someone in misery simply because his misery was poorly turned out. Yet this is precisely what we do in the case of fiction. If fictive woe wears a shabby suit we feel justified in shutting it out altogether.

This is, I think, just the reverse side of what we might dub Hume's paradox of tragedy. Hume in his small but characteristically penetrating essay 'Of Tragedy'[1] poses the question of why we enjoy tragedy precisely when it elicits strong emotions that would, in other contexts, be very painful. In Hume's words

> It seems an unaccountable pleasure which the spectators of a well-written tragedy receive from sorrow, terror, anxiety and other passions that are in themselves disagreeable and uneasy (p. 221).

Hume is clear that the tragedies we most value and enjoy are precisely those which provoke the strongest emotions:

> The more they (the spectators) are touched and affected the more are they delighted with the spectacle; and as soon as the uneasy passions cease to operate, the piece is at an end. One scene of full joy and contentment and security is the utmost that any composition of this kind can bear . . . (p. 221).

It might be thought that the answer to Hume's puzzle is quite straightforward: we are able to find the emotions of pity and terror agreeable because we don't really believe in what is transpiring on stage. Thus the stoic hopes to avoid all emotional commitment to the world by regarding it all as a play. Hume considers this option but dismisses it. For, he justly remarks, we may enjoy a tragedy even when we suppose that the represented events actually took place. He remarks of the epilogues of Cicero:

> The pathetic description of the butchery made by Verres of the Sicilian captains is a masterpiece. . . . (T)he sorrow here (is not) softened by fiction; for the audience were convinced of the reality of every circumstance (p. 224).

Inter alia, Hume rebuffs the idea that we enjoy such spectacles *simply* because they arouse emotions in us, for as he says 'being at a melancholy scene of that nature' would afford little entertainment.

Here the proponent of what we might call the doxastic solution to Hume's puzzle will naturally feel that Hume has misunderstood the force of his reply and is trading on an ambiguity. The relevant belief, the absence of which allows us to enjoy terror and pity, is not the belief that what is enacted before us took place once upon a time. Rather, it is the belief that what we are *now* seeing is the real article. It is proposed that one could then explain the lack of pain involved in watching a tragedy merely by adverting to the fact that people do not believe that what they are watching is the real thing. Disbelief is what takes the sting out of terror and pity.

However, such a response to Hume's puzzle would be obtuse for at least two reasons. First, this response simply does not answer Hume's question. Hume wanted to know why we enjoy tragedy. This response claims to do no more than explain why we don't regard the prospect of an evening at *King Lear* with fear and loathing. The question remains of why we find the excitation of normally painful emotions enjoyable or, to use Hume's word, 'delightful'. Indeed, given that normally unpleasant emotions are excited, it is hard to see how the doxastic solution to the puzzle can even explain the absence of pain in the audience. For surely, if the normally painful emotions are present, it has yet to be explained how they could fail to be painful in the theatre. If belief is relevant at all, it might explain why certain emotions are not aroused. (Hence the stoic's refusal to believe in the world: it frees him of emotional fetters; it doesn't merely take away the pain of wearing them.) But given that tragedy does arouse these painful emotions, in spite of our disbelief (empirically disconfirming the stoic's hope that disbelieving the world's existence would free us from emotion) it is very hard to see how mere disbelief in the spectacle could prevent the emotions it arouses from being painful ones.

There is a second, deeply systematic reason, why *Hume* could not help himself to the doxastic solution to his puzzle. For Hume, believing that *p* amounts to a particularly vivid idea or impression of *p*. And it could hardly be doubted that those tragedies we most enjoy are precisely those which come closest to giving us a lively picture of the events they relate. Hence there is a positive correlation between a tragedy's tendency to promote a belief in (or vivid idea of) what it relates and its tendency to promote our enjoyment. Such a positive correlation is, of course, the reverse of what the doxastic solution would predict.

Indeed, given Hume's equation of belief with lively ideas, it is very difficult to see how he can avoid the conclusion that we actually believe that what we see in the theatre is the real McCoy. Given that we are obviously aware that what we are seeing is not the genuine article, the best Hume could do would be to postulate a conflict among our beliefs. We would have, so his story might go, a lively idea of (and hence belief in) the fictive events but also a lively idea of (and hence belief in) the art and skill of the actors, costumiers, etc. These beliefs obviously conflict, but so what?

At any rate, the doxastic solution seems to be a poisoned pawn for Hume. Of course, in an age which piques itself on its sophisticated awareness of the agreeable possibilities of pain (thanks to von Sacher-Masoch) it might well be replied that Hume is just wrong to think that we do not feel pain when we witness a tragic spectacle. Perhaps we go there precisely in order to make ourselves feel pain. Perhaps tragedy is merely the sublimation of *le vice anglais*. Alternatively, perhaps it is just plain fun to watch suffering—perhaps we are all sadists *au fond*.

This reply contains an important truth, but it manifestly fails to solve Hume's puzzle, for even if it is true, as I think it is, that we feel, in some sense, pained by tragic spectacles, Hume is undoubtedly right that we find satisfaction in watching such spectacles. The fact that the experience is painful makes it more paradoxical, not less, that we find satisfaction in it. For let's face it, however much we preen ourselves on our open mindedness towards sado-masochism, there are few who would find satisfaction in watching a man running around with his eyes out (like Gloucester and Oedipus). So if we seek such experiences in the theatre, and we are neither unusually sadistic nor masochistic, this is something which invites an explanation.

Nor will it cut much ice simply to deny Hume's premise that we enjoy tragedy, for if we do not, the puzzle becomes curiouser and curiouser. If we don't even enjoy the thing, why on earth do we all flock to see it? Further-more, it cannot be doubted that we spontaneously accord the experience of high tragedy—painful and disturbing as it is—an intrinsic value. We don't need to be dragged to the theatre, after all. Of course, as a matter of social history, it is perhaps true that people in the eighteenth century had more stomach for gruesome entertainments than we have, and one might instance not only the pleasure taken by many in watching executions—akin perhaps to the frisson we experience in watching horror movies—but one might also instance the fashion for wearing one's hair à la victime (in imitation of the short cropped hair of the victims of the guillotine) that became the fashion in Directoire Paris. But I think we cannot dismiss Hume's puzzle as the relic of an age that enjoyed gore but refused to admit this to itself. The fact remains that *we* value and spontaneously seek the experience of watching in the theatre representations of what we would elsewhere avoid like the plague. And once we acknowledge this fact about ourselves, how can we help wanting to explain it to ourselves?

What was Hume's answer to his puzzle? Hume thought that the pleasure we take in the quality of the spectacle—the eloquent diction, the power of the acting, the beauty of the performers and their costume, the intrigue of the plot, and so on—simply overruled the pain we would normally feel in such situations.[2] Indeed, on Hume's view the painful emotions are transformed into pleasurable ones, apparently without loss of identity. Terror is no longer painful at all, but pleasurable.

Hume also saw what was wrong with this answer, though I think he did not see why he had to give the wrong answer—for seeing this would have shaken the foundations of Hume's account of reasons for action and value. Hume notes that if we are told of a real event, the sort of event a daily tabloid might call tragic, perhaps an event close to home, we would feel more pain and not less if the event were related to us in eloquent and moving free verse by someone dressed up like a messenger in a Greek play. This of course brings us right back to our starting point: we don't expect real woe to be tricked out in fancy dress and—what's more—we don't want it to be. Our taste in woe is, if you like, neo-classical; we like our woe neat. But then the problem is: why does eloquence counteract pain in the theatre but aggravate it in real life?

Hume tries to explain the asymmetry between the real and the theatrical emotions by claiming that in the theatre the aesthetic pleasure in the artifice is dominant and this pleasure transposes, as it were, the darker feelings into its key, while in the event of a real woe, the painful feelings toward the event are dominant and so would transform any pleasure in the style of presenting the grief into feelings of yet deeper pain. In each case, the dominant emotion is imperious, spreading itself onto the other emotions and harnessing them to its cause. However, Hume has signally failed to explain the asymmetry between the theatrical and real situations. *Why* is the aesthetic pleasure dominant in the theatre but subdued in the real life case? Surely this is virtually the same problem as the one with which we began.

But it is not *quite* the same problem, and this fact suggests a modest proposal. Namely, that the asymmetry be explained in terms of belief. The dominant emotions are those directed at states of affairs we take to be real. In the theatre, we know that our emotions are not excited by the real McCoy. The style of acting and eloquence of diction are quite real. So aesthetic pleasure gains the upper hand and the other emotions are transposed into the dominant key of aesthetic joy. In the event of a real woe, things are the other way around. The thing really happened and we believe it. Of course, if this event is eloquently related, we note this aesthetic fact. However, the reality of the woe simply overwhelms any aesthetic pleasure we might take and transform it into grief. Perhaps we might say that in the case of the actual grief, the vividness of our idea of the grief (which becomes, in Hume's account, grief) *absorbs* the vividness of our idea of the eloquence of the report, and so becomes a stronger grief. By contrast, in the fictive case, our *disbelief* in the event dampens our sympathetic grief but this sympathetic grief retains enough of its force to add a certain degree of liveliness to our idea of the theatrical representation.

Unfortunately, this solution is unavailable either to Hume or to ourselves. For one thing, most of us would reject the associationist theory of mental activity upon which Hume's answer is based (upon which the Humean component in the contrived answer is based). Hume's idea seems to be that the close proximity or temporal coincidence of the aesthetic feelings with emotions of, for example, terror and pity simply transforms the latter emotions into the pleasurable character of the former emotions. Yet both the explanantia—and perhaps most important of all—the explanandum seem wrong. The associationist framework is wholly discredited and the facts Hume here invokes it to explain would seem to admit of less tortured explanations. For example, it does seem right that thinking of something beautiful when you are in misery can make you more miserable. But mightn't this be explained in term of the *contrast* between that beautiful possibility and your present predicament? Doesn't this contrast serve at once to heighten the beauty of the object and the misery of your current state? And if an eloquent recital of the death of a loved one would be deeply mortifying, isn't this because we would feel such a recital to be both insincere and somehow an obstacle to a full absorption in our grief? Perhaps we resent anything which claims our attention when we are absorbed in some intense emotion. Indeed, we might find an eloquent recital of pleasant news equally irritating; it would not necessarily find favour with us thanks to its association with the good news. This, of course, heightens the mystery: why should the contrast be so little damaging to our satisfaction with tragedy, but so very disturbing to us in real life? The contrast between the beauty of the play, the acting and the actors on the one hand, and the misery of the characters represented on the other, does not seem to destroy our satisfaction in watching the play. Why should it do so in real life?

Yet, even if Hume's associationist framework were alright, and even if he were right that our terror in the theatre is anodyne (an assumption I will question shortly), he could not just tack on the doxastic solution to his own. I have already said that Hume could not easily accept any suggestion that we don't believe in the fictive events we see on stage. Given Hume's almost affective conception of what a belief consists in, what could be more a belief than our lively idea of Oedipus's fate? Indeed, Hume's account of sympathy[3] would almost seem to commit him to the view that belief is present in the case of our experience of Oedipus's fate. For according to Hume, sympathy is to be explained in the following way: we have a lively idea or impression of someone's expression, this in turn leads to a lively idea of the feeling expressed and this finally *becomes* something like the very emotion. Thus, our lively idea of Oedipus's pain and grief and horror tends to become those very emotions (obviously there are oddities here: we can have a conjunctive idea of pain, horror and happiness, but we can't have an experience which is at once all of these things). In any case, since we sympathise with Oedipus, we must have a lively enough idea of his fate to count as having a belief in its presence before us.

It might be suggested that this affective conception of belief is merely peculiar to Hume. I think not. I believe that we are dealing with an eighteenth century conception of what belief is.[4] The manuals of rhetoric and poetic composition suggest that it is one of the chief obligations of orator and poet to induce in his audience a lively image of the events he, as it were, depicts.[5] If the eighteenth century notion of belief is, as I think, precisely that of a lively image, then we can understand Coleridge's notion of 'willing suspension of disbelief' as neither metaphor nor nonsense, but (in intention at least) the literal truth. Furthermore, given this notion of belief as a kind of affect (a conception Hume clearly has and one which shows that it cannot be right to attribute to Hume, as John McDowell does, the separation of mind into cognitive and affective compartments)[6] we can understand why it is so important for Diderot that naturalistic art astonish, move and touch him. We might almost say that such feelings are criterial for belief. A spectacle that induces these strong emotions is therein judged by the spectator to be realistic (this is a thought to which I shall return).

In any case, given this conception of belief, which as it were dictates the form of the problem of tragedy for Hume and the eighteenth century, it is wholly ahistorical to insinuate a quite different notion of belief into the Humean solution. For us the problem is one of how we can attach value to tragedy given that (indeed because) it arouses unpleasant feelings in us. We will have to start from scratch if we want an answer to that question. Hume's associationist answer is no longer available to us.

It might appear that there is something in Hume's observation that the puzzle is to be solved by noting that in the theatre there are, as it were, two objects of attention: what is (fictively) happening and what is (really) happening (viz., how what is fictively happening is being represented). It might be said that in the theatre our pleasure stems from attending to how events are represented, not the events themselves.[7] We do of course attend to those events, and they excite painful emotions in us. But we are able to enjoy the experience of tragedy *despite* these painful emotions because (a) we enjoy attending to the style of the drama and the skill of the actors and (b) because we do not believe that what is represented as happening is happening. (We still need (b) to explain the asymmetry between the way style affects us in the theatre and the way it might affect us if we were told in rhyming couplets that our lover had just been killed.)

We might call this the mannerist solution. It suggests that we divide our attention between what is happening and how that is represented and that our pleasure in the tragic spectacle stems only from the latter and fortunately overcomes the pain which attends our response to the former. This solution fails to find a place either for the pleasure we take in the content of the tragedy or for the value we attach to our emotional responses to that content. It is not simply an incidental fact that fictional characters and their muddles excite our emotions. Rather, as Hume himself understood, this is the essence of tragedy: we attach value to the experience of tragedy precisely because of the emotions that it arouses in us. It is because these emotions are painful that there is, *prima facie*, a puzzle. Furthermore, this solution fails to take into account a possibility which disturbed some eighteenth century writers, such as Diderot: namely that too much attention to the representational vehicle might destroy the value the experience of tragedy has for us. Far from being a source of pleasure, obtrusive artifice can destroy the very value tragedy has for us. But on this proposed solution to Hume's puzzle—as indeed on Hume's solution—the artifice is the sole ground of the pleasure we take in tragedy; and if that is so, it is hard to see how one could get too much of it. There may be some things you can get too much of, but something which is supremely valuable isn't one of them.

Furthermore, Hume got the explanandum wrong. It seems just wrong to suggest that our reactions to fictive terrors do not retain their painful or disturbing character. Indeed, there is something almost nonsensical about the notion of a pain-free terror, even if it is an enjoyable one. It may be the very awfulness, terribleness, of the terror which we require for our satisfaction in the experience. In any case, it is just this type of logical connection, between painfulness and terror, which Hume's atomism ill equips him to appreciate. Indeed, I think the problem with Hume's view goes deeper than this. It is not just that he is wrong to suppose that terror and anxiety don't retain their painfulness in the theatre. He is even wrong to suppose that we always enjoy or find delight in the experience of tragedies. There may, of course, be some fictions which arouse terror in a way we find enjoyable—

ghost stories, monster films, films of violence. Here the experience seems to
be of a kind with the frisson of pleasure felt by the audience at an execution.
The terror is the product of the thought 'There but for the grace of God go I'
whereas the pleasure stems from the fact that we are not in fact ourselves in
the predicament. We congratulate ourselves on the contrast between
ourselves and the victim (we experience what Hobbes called 'sudden glory'). I
think we can see that such experiences have a quality and value quite
different from the quality and value attaching to the experience of tragedy.
The emotions involved—basically, terror tinged with self-congratulation—
are not admirable in themselves. Furthermore, the experience is enjoyed. By
contrast, when we contemplate the fate of Lear and Cordelia, the emotions
aroused are of a kind which we value, even though they are painful
emotions. We value the emphathetic terror and the sympathetic pity an
audience spontaneously feels in the contemplation of the fate of the
characters in a tragedy.

Hume, of course, could hardly acknowledge this possibility. *How* could we
accord value to such emotions, and therefore to the experience of tragedy
which induces such emotions, given that they are painful? Of course, Hume
could have given a reply of sorts here. He could have argued that the fact
that human beings harbour such emotions as pity and empathetic terror is a
fact which conduces to the benefit of mankind, since it tends to lead to
actions of succouring the distressed. In short, Hume might have appealed to
a kind of motive utilitarianism for help in dealing with this *prima facie*
objection to his hedonistic account of motivation and value. However, I think
all one can say is that the value accorded to the experience of tragedy seems
not to be of this utilitarian sort. Nor, indeed, could this provide an answer to
Hume's paradox, since we seem to seek in the theatre precisely those
emotionally disturbing experiences we elsewhere avoid. We do not take
account of the consequences of theatrical experience before valuing it—we
just value it. At the very least, that suggests that we are not, consciously at
least, utilitarian agents; we appear to ascribe an *intrinsic* value to disturbing
experiences. We *spontaneously* seek—without utilitarian forethought—
experiences painful in themselves which we nonetheless value. Now from
the standpoint of any hedonistic theory of value that must make our
behaviour seem at best recklessly irrational—at worst wicked. In any case, I
believe this allows us to reformulate our problem in a slightly crisper way.
The experience of tragedy is valued, and valued intrinsically, precisely
insofar as it arouses certain emotions (pity and empathetic terror) which are
disturbing. Furthermore, this experience is sought spontaneously. Our
seeking it is not irrational, not sadistic, not masochistic and not hypocritical.
By contrast, although we value our sympathetic responses to *actual* suffering
and woe, we do not seek to witness such suffering. Why not?

The question has now become why do we *seek* the experience of tragedy?
This remains paradoxical, even after we drop Hume's hedonistic conception
of value, because we seek in the theatre just those experiences which we
elsewhere do not seek. Now how are we to resolve this puzzle? It appears
that the solution must do *one or both* of two things. (1) One might attempt to

locate a value *peculiar* to tragedy, which does not attach to the witnessing of *actual* suffering, and which therefore explains why we seek the experience of tragedy but not the experience of watching real grief and suffering. (2) One might attempt to show that there is something particularly *bad* about seeking to witness actual suffering, but that there is nothing particularly bad about witnessing fictive or imaginatively represented suffering.

Before going further, we must take the opportunity to stamp out a couple of ambiguities. The first concerns the relation of the audience to the characters. Here, we must take care to compare like with like. For example, it won't do to contrast the fictive representation of a grief befalling someone unknown to the spectator with the experience of hearing about or witnessing a grief befalling someone near and dear to the spectator. Concerning someone near to the spectator, it is unlikely he would seek the experience either of hearing a play about or of witnessing a grief befalling him. However, the asymmetry remains concerning people to whom the spectator is not particularly related by any bonds of kinship or attachment: namely, that one would be willing to see a good play about his grief and suffering, but one would be reluctant in the extreme actually to witness his suffering.

Second, we must be clear that we are talking about *witnessing* a real sorrow, not simply hearing about it. That is, if someone is no relation to us, we are unlikely to feel particularly awful about hearing of his grief, though we should definitely not wish to witness it. Hume is of course correct that if someone is close to us, we should be vastly more pained by an eloquent recital of the news of his death than by a simple but sympathetic statement of the bare fact. However, if someone is not particularly close to us, an eloquent recital of their fate might be indistinguishable from a tragedy. What remains true, however, is that we should have no wish to witness their demise. But then, it would appear, Hume's objection to his own account simply vanishes. There *is* an asymmetry between a theatrical representation of suffering and the witnessing of it: for there is art in the former but no possibility of art in the latter. But we cannot let matters rest there, for as we have seen it is not only the presence of art in the theatrical representation which accounts for its value. It is the fact that something momentously awful is represented. Now if 'art' gives this representation value, we have yet to see why and in what sense this is so. Equally, in saying that the difference of import is that between seeing a theatrical representation of and actually witnessing grief and suffering, one is conceding that belief has some role to play in explaining why we freely go to theatrical tragedies but avoid actual suffering like the plague. However, it is as yet unclear *what* role the notion of belief plays in the overall resolution of the puzzle. The following roles are denied to it: disbelief does not prevent pity and terror, for we do react to the fate of tragic characters; nor does it transform painful emotions into pleasurable ones, for the experience of tragedy is far from being always delightful. Nor will it do to say that it is simply a primitive fact that we don't mind going to see disturbing fictive representations but we do mind witnessing events we believe to be occurring before us. For accepting this as primitive is just to give up the hope of deeper explanation. To be sure there is an asymmetry—of belief—and this seems to correlate with our choices: we seek the fictive emotions and avoid the factive one. But one feels that there ought to be more to it than that. *Why* should belief make this difference? And here, it is important to remember Hume's reminder that tragedies can be about real people. We can't, therefore, simply say that we permit ourselves to go to tragedies because it doesn't matter what happens in possible or fictive worlds, it only matters what happens here in the actual world. This can't be right, since tragedies are about the real world and can be about real people. What appears to matter is not the possible world involved, but our *point of view* on it. What matters is whether the event is before us, here, now. The belief that matters is, in David Lewis's jargon, a *de se* belief. It is not a belief that p, but a belief that 'I'm now seeing p', that is necessarily absent in the case of a theatrical representation of p. And in any case, the response that watching fictional characters suffer is alright because fictional characters are fictional and they don't matter is belied by the strong emotional response we give to them.

II

Now the very way we have formulated the puzzle seems to exclude a consequentialist solution. We do not typically value the tragic experience as a means to anything else, but rather accord it an intrinsic value. Since it is painful, and not necessarily at all pleasurable or delightful, it seems to present a counter-example to hedonistic theories of value—certainly to hedonistic theories of aesthetic value (such as those of Hume and indeed Kant). This cannot, as we have seen, be made good by averting to the pleasurable consequences arising from these painful experiences. If there are any such consequences, they have little to do with why we value the experience. More to the point, such character utilitarianism signally fails to solve the puzzle. For if we were to explain tragedy in terms of the hedonistic value to the human race of having the character of one who is compassionate and sympathetic, and even if we were to believe that going to tragedies could somehow develop such a character—rather than pre-supposing that one has such a sympathetic character—even after all these assumptions are granted in favour of the hedonistic response, two objections remain. The first is that if the consequentialist answer were correct, we would stop going to tragedies once we were satisfied with the character of our emotional dispositions (sensibilities). Yet it seems to me that there is nothing odd or irrational about someone of irreproachable sensibility attending a tragedy. Second, the consequentialist answer appears to me to offer no solution to the puzzle. For, if one had it in one's power to witness various *real* tragedies, one would not choose to do so, even on the off chance that it might be character-improving to do so. It should be stressed that these two problems would appear to arise for any consequentialist theory of our motivation in seeking the experience of tragedy. More generally, it must be conceded that consequentialism has nothing to offer a theory of aesthetic value.

The value of the experience of tragedy must be located *in* the experience of it. It is not something external to the experience. Therefore, we must look to that experience and ask what is valuable about it. The feature we hit upon must be a feature of those experiences of tragedy which we spontaneously seek. It must also be a feature which is precisely lacking in those experiences of witnessing real suffering and grief which we do not seek.

The traditional answer is that in tragedy, grief, suffering and other evils of human existence are made intelligible to us. They are seen as part of a natural order, a necessary and inevitable part. Tragedies end on a note of resolution. The natural order has been disturbed, and the tragedy moves ineluctably towards the restoration of that natural order. Sometimes—as with the crucifixion, the death of Socrates, the end of the *Oresteia*, the appearance of Fortinbras at the end of *Hamlet*—there is a hint of the advent of a *new* order. Of course, the moment of resolution is often the most horrible moment in the whole story, the moment at once most devoutly sought and devoutly feared. The Isenheim altarpiece makes the moment of the passion vividly real—yet it is not merely a moment of deep, bodily agony, it is also the moment which sees the birth of a new order among men, when the human race is left with the responsibility for setting its own house in order. We may now start from scratch, the world has been cleansed of the sin of Adam. Likewise, Hamlet—like a kind of Samson—carries the whole court of Denmark with him to the grave. Fortinbras arrives to assert a new order. What matters here is the belief in a universe that inevitably operates according to moral laws—the moral laws are treated as if they were natural laws (and it can be no accident that the tragic vision flourished in classical Greece and in the Renaissance at precisely those times when a notion of natural law informed men's expectations and hopes[8]). Given this belief, the tragedy is bearable. Indeed, can it plausibly be maintained that the devout Christian does not wish to witness the central event in the Church's history? The appropriate belief—in a kind of impersonal providence—would make the actual witnessing of the event bearable. For one with a belief in this world view, there could be no asymmetry between actually witnessing the tragic event and seeing it represented.

For those in command of the tragic view of life, there is no paradox of tragedy. There is no special question of why we witness in the theatre what we would elsewhere avoid. The tragic world view makes the sight of evil bearable, be it in the flesh or in the theatre. But we are not consoled by such a world view. There are bleak tragedies, tragedies that end on a note of wintry quiet, where the only consolation seems to be that life is finite, suffering must have an end—the story is almost over. This is the atmosphere of Schubert's song cycle *Die Winterreise*. The power of this cycle, its command of our rapt attention, cannot lie in any consoling vision of the world. On the contrary, winter has occupied the haunts of summer, and all that is left is reflection on the winter within the poet's soul—reflection, wandering, madness and death. The power of such an experience must reside in the intimacy of it. We do not witness the suffering from without, but rather from within the very soul of the sufferer. The value we attach to this experience and the reason we seek it is undoubtedly just this: that it gives us an imaginative sense of what it is like to feel, see and live in a certain way. No mere perception of grief from without could give us so strong a sense of the subjective reality of grief.

Yet, in some ways this must make it seem more paradoxical, not less, that we seek the experience of such wintry epiphanies. For, if I am right, they bring us closer to the vivid soul of grief, they offer no consoling promise of anything more than a release from the grip of grief in the metamorphosis from being someone into being nothing. The *loss* of subjectivity—in madness or death—seems to be the only escape from pain. This appears to be the bad news in *King Lear*, and in the *Winter Journey*. But why do we seek such news? Because, I think, many people feel that that is how things are and that it is better to know how things are than not to know. (An intuition that Nozick makes vividly clear to us with his experience machine.[9]) In the experience of a work of art, we are allowed to witness this fate, our fate, from within the experience of another. It is this quality which calls forth our empathetic emotions—emotions of pity and terror. And this is emphatically not like watching someone else suffer—it is an experience in which we realise that when the character speaks of his experience, he is speaking with the 'universal voice'. We are reminded vividly that men are not islands—it is one of the bonds uniting us that we imaginatively share in fates that are not yet ours, but may be soon.

What is the difference, then, between the experience of such high tragic art and watching a real person go mad? The difference is in the intimacy of the experience—by imaginatively realising his character, the author has made an experience available to us as it were from within, on the most intimate footing.

I think we can provide something like an argument for the intuition that it is the *reality* of this suffering that commands us to witness it. I think we often feel that we are justified in watching certain films because—*but only because*—things are actually like that. There would be no justification in watching *fantasies* of torture and mass murder. But because these moral enormities are a fact of our lives we allow—we force—ourselves to witness them in films and photographs.

It might be objected that this is a consequentialist theory of the value of tragedy. We see it as adding to our store of knowledge of the world, and this is valuable to us for various reasons. But the fact is that there appears to be little of value in these revelations over and above the experience of them. Very often, there is nothing we can do about the 'facts' they force us to witness. True, it may be argued that watching a film about Auschwitz may have an effect on an audience—it may make them resolve that 'never again' shall such things happen. But the value we attach to the experience does not seem to reside solely in this possible upshot—it appears to reside in the revelation of atrocity, the revelation itself and nothing else.

It might be asked: if it is the revelation you seek, and nothing else, why not seek out experiences of actual suffering? The answer seems to be that such experiences cannot be as intimate as theatrical experience (unless of course we know the sufferer—but we have excluded this possibility). The theatre allows us an intimate contact with the suffering of another. Such contact would be impossible in real life, since sufferers are too absorbed in grief to give a running commentary—and if they do provide such a commentary, such an 'expression' in Collingwood's sense, then perhaps we might say that in some sense they are artists with a claim on our attention.

In any case, someone truly absorbed in grief cannot make the experience of that grief available to us (he may do so after the fact in a work of art, of course). This impossibility is overcome in the theatre—there we are allowed to see into the grief and other extreme emotions of others. The characters and their experiences are present to us but we are not present to them (we do not interfere with their grief). Of course, I am not merely adverting to the fact that the characters are *not aware* of us (though various devices in the theatre and painting are used to underline this fact). Rather, their expressions and actions have been conceived by a controlling intelligence that would not be available to an ordinary mortal in extreme states of emotion.[10]

I have suggested that tragedy makes possible for us something which is not possible outside of imaginative experience: the vivid, powerful realisation of what it is like to suffer (and of course art makes available more positive emotions to us as well). This knowledge is apparently of a very peculiar kind—it is an end in itself (although it may also be valuable for other purposes). Nor does it seem to be cumulative. We do not ever get the feeling, 'Now I know enough about human suffering, about what it is like to suffer. I shall no longer go to see tragedies.' Real suffering cannot be expressed by the sufferer in a way that makes a vivid and powerful impact on our understanding—precisely because anyone who is really in the throws of a powerful emotion hasn't got the necessary control over himself to make his experience available to us (also because our presence would necessarily alter the state of anyone aware of it). The artist, of course, possesses the controlling intelligence which allows his characters to act before us and speak to us in a way which makes their suffering unforgettable. This, of course, brings us back to the starting point of the essay: our reaction to fictional characters is not just a reaction to fictional people, it is a reaction to them *as represented* in the text (on stage, in the movie, etc). Therefore, our reaction is necessarily governed by *how* they are represented, and the kind of emotion that it is appropriate to feel is determined by the quality of the representation. Where little controlling intelligence has been exercised, where the people are treated virtually as found objects, then we may feel that it is inappropriate to respond emotionally to them (as represented). One of the *pleasures* (and here I think this is the right word) of seeing a tragedy, however bleak, stems from our interaction with the controlling intelligence of the artist. The characters to whom we react or fail to respond are the product of that intelligence and our reactions constitute a kind of judgment of his work—of him insofar as he manifests himself in his work. Thus, we are reacting to characters as vividly seen and realised by a controlling intelligence and we respond to the work as an expression of that achieved vision of the characters. It is an important fact about our reaction to the suffering of actual people that our emotional reaction to their suffering does not constitute, even in part, a judgment on their expression of suffering. We simply cannot expect real suffering to permit this kind of control over expression. There is a natural feeling that if such control was exercised, the expression could not be quite sincere. Far from making the suffering more real, such control would make it seem less real. Paradoxically, the opposite is the case in the theatre. Suffering is made more real by artifice. There is no real paradox, though, since the artifice is that of the artist and not the character.

III

Fictions, as I began by saying, can have a claim on our emotions. What kind of failure is it in a work not to justify this claim? What kind of failure is it in us not to respond to a justified claim? I think that we can clarify this by comparing our emotional reactions to fictions with judgments of taste.

On Kant's view, a judgment of taste, which takes the canonical form 'x is beautiful', is necessitated neither by our understanding of x nor by anything about x relevant either to morality or prudence. Aesthetic judgment is a kind of pleasure which is free or independent of the claims of understanding and morality. Kant calls such judgments 'disinterested' by which he means, not indeed that we do not find the objects of our aesthetic favour interesting, engaging or absorbing, but rather that this engagement is dictated neither by our understanding nor by practical reasoning. Yet, though an aesthetic judgment cannot claim to be justified by understanding or morality alone, it must claim the agreement of others. What distinguishes an aesthetic judgment of the form 'x is beautiful' from the mere fact that x pleases me is that fact that I refer my pleasure in x to the 'universal voice'. In other words, I not only find x pleasant, but I think others ought to find x pleasant as well. Kant seems to suggest that we refer our judgment not to our common understanding or to a common set of interests and duties, but rather to the free play of such faculties as we all have in common.

It might be helpful to reflect that the emotion of love is formally analogous to a Kantian judgment of taste.[11] Our love for someone is not dictated by what we understand about him, nor is it ever dictated by morality (either considered as duty or considered as involving such feelings as compassion and beneficence: we do not bestow our love 'dutifully' or 'compassionately'). Nor is love—it cannot logically be—dictated by our interests, by the fact that a person can be useful in a certain way. The difference between love and a judgment of taste is that we do not refer our love to the universal voice: I do not think it is any part of our love for someone that we demand of everyone that they too shall love him, though we may very well make this demand on a small community (our friends).

Now it seems to me that there is a similar structure to the picture of our emotional responses to fictional characters. Imagine what we should say about someone who didn't share our emotional attachments and responses to the characters in, say, *Emma*. Suppose I say that I think Mr Woodhouse a tiresome old fool. And someone says, 'He's merely a fictional character, a verbal construct. You treat him as though he were real'. What am I to say? A less radical disharmony of sentiment might prevail. Someone might fail to feel what I feel without feeling nothing at all. But whether disagreement be global or local, the question arises of what we are to say about the disagreement between our responses.

I want to suggest that when we react to characters in a fiction our response is based neither upon understanding nor morality alone, but nonetheless we expect people to share our response. We think something is amiss when someone doesn't share our response to a fictional character. But, as with judgments of taste, we cannot refer our disagreement to the arbitration of understanding and morality. Someone who does not share our emotional response to a fiction may yet understand the text as well as we do and be as nice a person as we are. Our emotional response to fiction is not supervenient upon our understanding or our morality. Hence, our responses are freely given or 'disinterested' in Kant's sense. This suggests to me that our responses to fictions are instances of judgments of taste.[12] We don't merely respond to fiction, we feel also that certain responses are in order while others are out of order. A 'sentimental' work is one which lays claim to more of an emotional response from us than it has a right to extract.

Now, of course, I have said that many of our emotional responses to fictional characters and their situations may be unpleasant and disturbing. Thus, our hatred of Iago and fear for Desdemona are far from being delightful experiences. Yet, they do seem to be tinged with a kind of pleasure. I think we may refer this to the fact that our responses to fictional characters are always responses to them as represented. Thus, our hatred of Iago is a kind of tribute to the work. We acknowledge that it has the power to extract this emotion, and we think it ought to extract this emotion. We admire and delight in the character *as* Shakespeare's creation, but we despise him as a man. This duality in the object of our response might be compared to our perception of an object in a painting where we simultaneously admire the brushwork and form various feelings about the depicted object. One should distinguish one's aesthetic response to the painting from one's aesthetic response to the fictive object. The painting of something ugly may elicit the judgment—directed at the object *in* the painting—'That's ugly'. But eliciting this judgment of the depicted object may be a triumph of the painter's skill. Thus, the painting finds favour with us in virtue of being able to elicit such a (negative) aesthetic judgment of the depicted object. I do not mean that we would necessarily call the painting of such an ugly object beautiful, probably we would not. Now I think something like this is going on in *Lear* or *Die Winterreise*. The emotions which the dramatic personae of these works call forth are uniformly disturbing and upsetting. Yet, the very fact that such emotions are called forth—and ought, we feel, to be called forth—makes us think all the more highly of the play.

But I do want to stress that our emotional reaction to the characters is not something you can analyse out of our overall reaction to the work (another way of putting this would be to say that the aesthetic pleasure in the work is not something you can analyse out of our emotional reactions to the characters as represented). That is why I say that these reactions are, in effect, judgments of taste.

Now if this is right, if our emotional reactions to fictions count as Kantian judgments of taste, then I think a purely formalistic reading of Kant's aesthetic must bite the dust (of course, I don't wish to imply that any such misreading is now prevalent among Kant scholars). For in the case of our emotional responses to fiction (be it poetry, music or painting) we have something which is clearly directed to the content of the work but which counts (on an extension of Kant's view) as an aesthetic judgment. This implies, of course, that understanding a work may be a necessary condition of an appropriate aesthetic response. A Kantian need merely maintain that it is not a sufficient condition. This view also suggests an obvious way in which a recognisably Kantian view of aesthetic judgments need not be amoralistic, since a fiction may lay claim to our moral emotions and so certain emotional dispositions (of a moral sort) may be necessary for the correct response to a fiction. (Kant, of course, had notorious difficulty in finding a place for moral emotions in his moral philosophy, due, I think, primarily to the value he placed upon autonomy. There is some hope that an Aristotelian view of sensibility might make the value we ascribe to being properly affected by certain events compatible with the intuition we have that morally relevant features of a person must be features for which he is responsible.)

What is it that someone lacks who doesn't respond emotionally to deserving fictions? Evidently, he need lack neither understanding nor moral decency. So we say he lacks taste and imagination. Both of these are problematic answers however. I think we must resist the temptation to think that by saying of someone that he lacks taste and imagination we are some-how *explaining* his response by postulating faculties of taste and imagination which one person has and another person lacks. Such an explanation would have little more value than the explanation of the sleep inducing properties of opium in terms of a *virtus dormitiva*. Of course, when we say someone lacks taste or imagination, we suggest that there is a dispositional fact about him, a fact in virtue of which he quite generally fails to respond as we do in various contexts. But there seems to be nothing more to someone's lacking taste than the fact that he does not, generally, respond as we do in certain contexts. He is not an *unsereiner*, not one of 'the happy few'. He is not a member of a particular community of imaginative sentiment.

I think this is an important fact. When we say someone lacks taste, it is not so much that we are making an accusation against him as that we exclude him from a certain community. If you will, we shame him. He lacks the grace to give freely and liberally those emotional responses which we, in our fortunate group, bestow on certain works. He is not unlike someone who understands—and perhaps even gives dispassionate approval to—some ceremony, such as the Royal Wedding, but simply does not respond emotionally like those who 'verstehen' the ceremony. He may understand the ceremony perfectly in a 'thin' sense of understand. He may think it a good thing. He just fails to respond like other members of the community, and so he is felt to be not quite 'one of us'.

I should emphasise, that in saying that an emotive response to fictional characters and their predicaments doesn't necessarily follow from an understanding and correct moral appreciation of those characters and their situations, I do not want to imply that such responses are other than *natural*. It might very well be that such responses are natural, and not artificial. It may be, rather, that someone who is globally unable to respond as we do to fictions holds some perverse view (such as a structuralist view of literature) which obliges him to refrain from emotional attachments to fictional characters.

I must also qualify another assertion I have made: that someone who *understands* a novel, a character or a song as well as we do might still fail to react as we do. Clearly there is a rather thin sense of 'understand' that makes such a divergence of sentiment possible even among those who comprehend the work equally.[13] Thus, someone might do quite well on tests intended to gauge the ability of the reader to understand the words and sentences in the text. But his understanding in this thin sense may have left him 'cold'. One might feel, however, that there is a richer sense of understanding according to which it would be right to say that anyone deprived of the appropriate emotional responses to a fictional situation simply does not understand that situation—in rather the way someone suffering some grief might feel that only those who empathise with him can really be said to understand his sorrow. Certain emotional reactions—of admiration (for courage, fairness, moderation), respect (for self-sacrifice), pity and sympathy (for suffering and grief)—may be said to be *criterial* for this kind of understanding. This carries over into the imaginative and fictive realm: one who lacks pity for Gloucester has simply not seen the point. This I believe is why a work representing people and their passions—for the *pour soi* is, as it were, the formal object of 'Verstehen'—is only fully realistic if it succeeds in making us feel that the characters as represented deserve the same emotional response as real people in similar situations would deserve. If this is right, then the notion of a work's being realistic is necessarily something that we can apply to a work only in virtue of an understanding of it in this richer sense. Of course, with second order *Verstehen* as with first order *Verstehen*, someone without the appropriate reactions might nonetheless apply the terms—'realistic', etc.—correctly. But the same point would arise at the second order level—namely that if the terms were not attached to the work in virtue of our emotional reactions to it, the point of the term, of the kind of art for which it stands, would simply have been missed.

Though I have stressed that these two kinds of understanding may fall apart, in that someone may understand a work in the thin sense without comprehending it in the richer sense, I do not mean to suggest that these two kinds of understanding are phenomenologically separable for the man of taste and imagination. For him, to understand just is to understand in the richest sense possible. He just could not see the features of the work which one is required to see in order to count as understanding it in the thin sense without feeling those sentiments which are criterial for understanding in the richer sense. It is not as if there is some special exertion of the imagination or of some special power of taste involved in his emotional apprehension of the work. For the man of taste, his sympathy, compassion, pity, terror, hate and love for fictive beings *is* supervenient upon his understanding. This is to be compared to the reactions of the virtuous man. For him, to understand suffering in the thin sense *is* to understand it in the richer sense.

IV

We now have the last ingredient that we require for the ultimate disposition of Hume's paradox of tragedy. Hume saw that we value tragedy precisely for its power to disturb, move and touch us; originally his question was of why we should find such experiences, normally in themselves disagreeable, so delightful in the theatre. Given Hume's picture of the problem—how do unpleasant experiences become pleasant—Hume's solution is perhaps the right one; he is perhaps correct to point to our appreciation of mimetic artifice and decorative diction as the source of our pleasure in tragedy. However, I have found a different problem, and this is: Why should we find these theatrical experiences *valuable* when we should normally think it irrational, sentimental, masochistic or sadistic to seek an experience of this disturbing kind? Given that the experience is unpleasant, why is it not irrational to seek it? Given that tragedy involves the extortion of powerful emotions, why is it not mere sentimentality to indulge in it? Given that it involves the vivid imagination of someone's suffering, why is not tragedy merely sadistic?

The answer I have offered is that the representation of suffering—and other extreme states—proposes an understanding of what it is like to suffer that is simply unavailable to the witness of actual suffering by reason of the fact that the actual sufferer cannot fashion his actions into a powerful expression of his experience. When the sufferer is able to overcome his suffering to the extent of being able to communicate and express it to us, he thereby establishes a claim on our aesthetic regard (and our reluctance to heed his expressions can only be the result of squeamishness). This suggests that the natural division is not the one between the experience of real suffering and the experience of theatrical depictions of suffering; the real division of moment is between our witnessing the symptoms of suffering (or some other extreme state of mind) and our witnessing its *expression* (in Collingwood's sense).

What then is the reason why the *disturbing* emotional quality of tragedy should contribute to rather than detract from its value? If the value of tragedy lies in its capacity to convey a vivid sense of what it is like to undergo various human fates, why is not its power to arouse disturbing emotions in us merely an incidental and unfortunate by-product of the experience? But the sceptic here fails to reckon with the point we have established in the last section: that *Verstehen* and sympathy are inseparable; the connection between the fact of understanding what it is like to go mad and the fact of being moved by this fate is not contingent but rather 'grammatical'. One might put it this way: the criteria by which we judge that someone has understood Lear's fate essentially include the criteria by which we judge that he has been moved by Lear's fate. Make-believe *Verstehen*, like literal or actual *Verstehen*, is conceptually linked to certain emotional responses. Hume himself attempted to depict this fact as a mental process in his account of sympathy, which has the mind move from an impression of a man's behaviour to an idea of the feelings which cause the behaviour and from thence, by association with the idea of the self that has been utilised in making the transition from the behaviour to the feeling, the mind moves from an idea of someone else's feeling into that very state of feeling. Hume's account of sympathy is perhaps a bit crude, but in it resides his best answer to his paradox of tragedy.

NOTES

1 David Hume, *Essays, Moral, Political and Literary* (Oxford, 1963). All page references in the text are to this edition.

2 The general mechanism whereby normally painful experiences cause associated pleasurable experiences to become even more pleasurable than they would be without the association is discussed by Hume in the *Treatise*, Bk II, Pt III, Sect iv.

3 For Hume's account of sympathy see *Treatise*, Bk II, Pt 1, Sect xi.

4 On Hume's own account there should be no particular asymmetry between belief and emotion; a vivid belief can cause an emotion (as in the mechanism of sympathy) and equally an idea can become vivid and so a belief) by association with a feeling. Jane Austen describes the latter process in *Sense and Sensibility*: '. . . (W)hat Marianne and her mother conjectured one moment, they believed the next—with them to wish was to hope, and to hope was to expect.' For the suggestion that Hume's use of 'sentiment' to cover both belief and emotion may have influenced later writers see R F Brissenden's ''Sentiment': Some Uses of the Word in the Writings of David Hume' in R F Brissenden (ed.), *Studies in the Eighteenth Century* (Canberra, 1968).

5 See for example Kames's *Elements of Criticism* (1762).

6 It seems to me that Davidson's attempt to recruit Hume for the 'cognitivist' cause in 'Hume's Cognitive Theory of Pride' (reprinted in D Davidson, *Essays on Actions and Events* (Oxford, 1980) must fail or at least be very misleading; for if Hume has a cognitive theory of indirect passions, it is equally clear that he has a sentimental or affective conception of belief (cf. *Treatise*, Bk I, Pt III, Sect viii). To someone who holds a cognitive theory of emotion, in which, for example, the belief that something awful is going to happen is an essential component in fear, it must seem a paradox that terror and pity are felt at all in the theatre; by contrast, the problem for Hume is twofold: Given the potential vivacity of theatrical experience, is it not the case that we believe in the reality of what is represented? and Given our intense reactions to tragedy, why is the experience nonetheless pleasing?

7 Arthur Danto intimates such a solution in his *Transfiguration of the Commonplace* (Cambridge, Mass., 1981), p. 23.

8   The traditional view of tragedy is well expounded by Northrop Frye, *Anatomy of Criticism* (Princeton, 1957), pp. 206-23.

9   Nozick's experience machine fiction proposes a choice between two hedonically equivalent streams of experience, one stream being veridical and the other being produced by an experience machine. Nozick argues that since we would prefer the veridical stream to the manufactured stream, we place a value on knowledge of how things *really are*. If I am right, the value we place on disturbing tragic spectacles reinforces the same point. John Skorupski drew the parallel to my attention. Cf. R Nozick, *Anarchy, State and Utopia* (New York, 1974), pp. 42-5.

10   The classical source for these theories is Diderot's *Paradoxe sur le comédien*, where he argues that the actor cannot actually feel the emotions of the character, because if he felt them he would be less effective in depicting them. See also the useful study by Michael Fried, *Absorption and Theatricality: Painting and Beholder in the Age of Diderot* (Berkeley, 1980). I have lifted the term 'controlling intelligence' from Colin Lyas's paper in this collection.

11   These thoughts were inspired by reading Ted Cohen's paper 'Why Beauty is a Symbol of Morality', now published in T Cohen and P Guyer (eds), *Essays in Kant's Aesthetics* (Chicago, 1982).

12   My remarks on the parallel between emotional responses to fiction and judgments of taste owe much to Ted Cohen's analogy between judgments of taste and finding the fun in a joke; see his paper 'Jokes' in Eva Schaper (ed.), *Pleasure, Preference and Value: Studies in Philosophical Aesthetics* (Cambridge, forthcoming).

13   My notion of 'thick' and 'thin' understanding derives from Clifford Geertz's 'Thick Description: Toward an Interpretative Theory of Culture' in his *The Interpretation of Cultures* (London, 1975).

VI

THE CENSORSHIP OF WORKS OF ART

R W Beardsmore

When Hume remarked 'generally speaking the errors in religion are danger-ous, those in philosophy only ridiculous',[1] he was expressing what is on the whole a fairly recent view of philosophy. Certainly it is not a view which would have recommended itself to those Athenians who put Socrates to death for corrupting the youth. And one might be tempted to attribute it to a peculiarly Anglo-American view of the relevance of the arts and humanities to everyday life. I think that it was Peter Ustinov who once countered a television interviewer's complacent remarks about the tolerance of the West towards its poets and novelists with the suggestion that the correct name for this 'tolerance' is 'indifference'. In Russia, he observed, they may indeed censor the work of their greatest writers, but there is a also a town called Gorki. There is no Dickenstown in England, nor to the best of my knowledge a Clemenstown in America.

Nevertheless it would be ungenerous to suggest that the popularity of Hume's view among present-day philosophers is due simply to indifference to the humanities, and perhaps rather too generous to Hume to attribute it solely to his own influence. For one reason why there has been a tendency, especially in this country, for philosophers to fight shy of any attempt to use philosophy to criticise human institutions is the influence, or assumed influence, of a far greater philosopher; I mean Ludwig Wittgenstein.

In *Philosophical Investigations*, *On Certainty* and elsewhere, Wittgenstein warns against the danger of supposing that there are certain language-games which are a necessary feature of the life of *any* society. We can, he suggests, imagine people who have no counterparts to ways of speaking which are fundamental in our society. Nor can it be demonstrated that these people's language would be deficient. Since any language-game is based on ways of acting for which reasons are neither required nor possible, it follows that language-games can neither be justified by reasons, nor rejected by showing that they are irrational.

Now much of what we make of this argument will depend on what we take Wittgenstein to have meant by a language-game. And if, like, for example, Thomas Morawetz in his book *Wittgenstein and Knowledge*, we take Wittgenstein to mean simply *any* practice in which men engage,[2] we shall swiftly be led to the conclusion that philosophy is irrelevant to human life.

Philosophy can neither justify nor criticise language-games; all human practices are language-games; *ergo* . . . .

Whether Wittgenstein intended it or not, the conclusion which I have suppressed on the ground of obviousness is palpably false. In our own society, judging people's character by their birth signs and employing alleged psychic powers to foretell the future are fairly common practices and are often taken seriously. Yet it is clear that both are vulnerable to philosophical argument. For, in the case of the former it is easy enough to show that, though self-styled astrologers commonly assess my character having been told my date of birth, no one ever responds to the challenge to estimate my date of birth from an assessment of my character, and that consequently any claim to a unique correlation between the two is without justification. And in the case of the latter, it is noticeable that claims to foreknowledge are always either of such generality as to be impervious to falsification or are simply reinterpreted or ignored where they turn out to be false. A Dallas housewife with alleged psychic powers recently claimed to have foreseen the assassination of President Reagan. She was, it turned out, over a month out in her prediction so that by the time Hinckley's shots were fired, she had decided that the psychic warning referred to the death of her own brother some weeks earlier. Even if we ignore the obvious difficulty that the President was not, as we now know, assassinated, it is still obvious that *someone* will die at least every month, especially in Dallas.

True, any philosopher will be well-advised to use arguments of this sort with caution. For confused sceptical attacks on human institutions are considerably more common in our history than are confused human institutions so that it is a counsel of prudence to suspect the argument rather than an institution, especially where the institution is itself part of an alien culture where the risk of misunderstanding is great, or like religion is a part of our own culture but one which many find difficulty in understanding.

Nevertheless, whatever Wittgenstein and some of his followers may have thought, there is no reason why a human practice, even a relatively common one should not rest on confusion, and in this paper I hope to show that one practice which is of considerable importance, and perhaps even fundamental to the maintenance of certain kinds of social order, is a case in point. I have in mind the practice of censoring works of art.

I

In our society the issues of censorship seems more naturally to arise in connection with works of literature and to some extent films. There is, I suppose, no necessity about this. Plato after all held that music could corrupt, and paintings as well as books have been banned. Still it ought not to be surprising that many people see art as a threat, which it is tempting either to ignore or suppress. For, though an important part of our lives, it is also a force which may sometimes lead us to question those things which we simply take for granted. Taking things for granted is not, of course, to be seen as simply a regrettable tendency which rational men would do well to eradicate, as many philosophers have implied. It is, as Wittgenstein emphasised in his later writings, a precondition of the possibility of rational thought itself.

> Lavoisier makes experiments with substances in his laboratory and then concludes that in combustion such and such happens. He does not say that of course another time it might happen differently. He goes by a particular world-view, and of course he has not invented this but learned it is what goes without saying as the foundation of his research, and this is also why it is never mentioned.[3]

We could not say that Lavoisier was careless or slipshod because he did not question or perhaps even notice this feature of scientific method, nor is it something which a more careful approach in science might show to be simply mistaken. For unless a man *does* take it for granted that results obtained on different occasions under laboratory conditions will be uniform and that they will have a significance outside the laboratory, then we shall not understand what is meant by 'laboratory conditions' or by an experiment. What Wittgenstein describes as a feature of Lavoisier's world-picture is something without which *any* sort of scientific method would be impossible and without which any talk of scientific error would lack sense. It is not, as writers like Russell have sometimes suggested, a mere assumption which must be questioned if our knowledge is to rest on secure foundations.

There will be many things which we take for granted in other areas of our lives, in morality, religion, mathematics, too and were this not so, various aspects of the way in which we discuss these things would also lose their sense. But the example that Wittgenstein gives may be misleading when we turn to consider other cases. For while it is difficult, if not impossible, to imagine anything which might lead scientists to give up the sort of assumption of uniformity which Wittgenstein mentions, what this shows is that there need be nothing idle or irrational in taking things for granted, and that it would itself be a confusion to think of these things as simple errors or mistakes not that what is taken for granted can *never* be questioned. And it is here that art may have a part to play in bringing to light and challenging what is taken for granted. Let me give an example.

When in 1971 Francis Ford Coppola's film *The Godfather* was released, it was so only after considerable public protest and in the face of many attempts, some of them involving acts of physical violence, to suppress the film. Part of the reason for this public reaction stemmed, as is well known, from the feeling that the film constituted a slur on the Italian-American community, but another objection which I have commonly heard made is that Coppola presents violence as a natural and indeed inescapable response in certain sorts of social situation, and ultimately shows violence as triumphing over the forces of justice.

Now it is interesting that in this respect *The Godfather* can scarcely compare for sheer sadism with several other films released over the past few years—*Straw Dogs*, *The Exorcist*, *Soldier Blue*—which, though lacking much redeeming artistic merit, did not draw as much adverse public comment (or if, as in the case of *The Exorcist*, they did, did so for rather different reasons). Nor is it hard to see why. Part of the reason is illustrated by the tendency of many people to talk of violent crime and perhaps of crime in general as a 'problem', to speak of the 'problem of the violent offender', to suggest methods of ridding society of the criminal element, to advocate a return of 'law and order', and so on. What is generally presupposed by these ways of talking is the notion, never explicitly stated but rather taken for granted, that it is possible to locate in *any* sort of society an area of activity which is criminal or unjustifiably violent and which be distinguished from what is not criminal, or if violent, then justifiably so. Now like any work of art *The Godfather* does not state that this notion must be rejected. Rather, it portrays, through the life of Don Vito Corleone and his family, and in particular through the constantly frustrated attempts of his son Michael to escape from the life of the Mafia only to be forced back into crime by a corrupt police force, racial prejudice, the indifference of law-abiding citizens, that there may be sorts of society, so shot through with corruption that the distinction between the criminal and the forces of law and order is an unreal or perhaps pointless distinction, and where fundamental injustices (racial prejudice, economic inequality) are so much a part of the fabric of the society that it is merely idle to distinguish the just man from the unjust man. Obviously, to the advocate of law and order or a strengthening of the arm of the law as an 'answer' to the 'problem' of crime, such a suggestion, if it is not merely ignored will be a disturbing one. And so it is not surprising if one response is to attempt to suppress the suggestion. As G K Chesterton once remarked, 'If you make any sentient creature jump, you render it by no means improbable that it will jump on you.' Nevertheless, though natural, it by no means follows that the reaction is a rational one. To show this let us begin by examining some of the forms which this reaction may take.

In 1898 Count Leo Tolstoi completed the essay called *What is Art?* in which, notoriously, he issues a blanket condemnation of some of the most respected works of arts of his, or indeed of any, time. Claiming to judge art from the standpoint of the 'religious perception', that is the prevailing moral ideal, of his age, Tolstoi notes that one after another alleged masterpiece stands condemned because it neither transmits feelings of love for God and one's neighbour, nor transmits feelings which 'unite men in the joys and sorrows of life'.

> "What, the Ninth Symphony not a good work of art?"
> I hear exclaimed by indignant voices.
> And I reply: Most certainly it is not.[4]

The conclusion Tolstoi thinks, is obvious. Bad art 'deserves not to be encouraged but to be driven out, denied and despised' and 'the efforts of those who wish to live rightly should be directed towards the destruction of this art'.[5] Tolstoi's essay was itself censored in several Russian versions before its publication in its original form in English.

Almost fifty years later, George Orwell who had himself condemned Tolstoi's views as 'worthless' reviewed Salvador Dali's *Secret Life*, an autobiography with illustrations drawn by Dali. Dali's work, Orwell remarks, is 'a direct, unmistakable assault on sanity and decency; and even—since some of Dali's pictures would tend to poison the imagination like a pornographic postcard—on life itself'.[6] And this is apparently at least a *prima facie* case for saying that the book should be censored. True, Orwell thinks that Dali's work casts a useful light on the decay of capitalist civilisation and for this reason it would be 'doubtful policy' to suppress it. But it is clear that for Orwell the case for refraining from censorship is one that has to be made. Just as a wall may be a good wall and yet deserve to be demolished if it surrounds a concentration camp, 'so it ought to be possible to say, "This is a good book or a good picture and it ought to be burned by the public hangman." ' What is again of interest here is that the essay *Benefit of Clergy* was itself subsequently suppressed on the grounds of obscenity.

Now, though these two cases, cases in which the prospective censor is himself the subject of censorship, would be just the kind which would in ordinary parlance be called 'paradoxical', there is in fact no genuine logical paradox involved. We can, that is to say, describe what transpired without contradiction, either explicit or implicit. Still, there is something about the institution of censorship which has led some writers to ask whether it does not involve some form of conceptual oddity, whether there is not some confusion involved in, to use Orwell's own example, the attempt to infer from, 'This is a morally evil book or picture' to the conclusion, 'This book or picture ought to be burned'.

Of these undoubtedly the most famous is John Stuart Mill in his essay *On Liberty*. Like many political philosophers before and after him Mill's aim is to outline the 'nature and limits of the power which can be legitimately exercised by society over the individual', but for my purposes what is important is a corollary which Mill draws from his own account of these limits. For one thing about which Mill is clear is that any interference with freedom of expression, any form of censorship, is well outside them. Though Mill's argument is complex, it can, I think, without parody be said to rest on the claim common to empiricists from Locke to Ayer that, since it is possible to imagine circumstances in which *any* judgment whatsoever may turn out to be false,[7] there are no judgments whose truth can be claimed to be certain. We can never attain certainty in our judgments, only satisfy ourselves that so far as possible we have considered and shown to be false any contrary judgments. But, this being so, it follows that censorship can never be justified, since of its nature it removes the conditions under which such a process is possible. If the judgment we censor is true, then we are left with error. If the judgment which we censor is erroneous, we are left with what is as bad, a judgment which, because we cannot know how it will fare in the face of contrary evidence, can never be *known* to be true. And to rest content with such a judgment is to be satisfied with mere convention and dogma.

It would be a mistake to underestimate the initial plausibility of Mill's argument, a plausibility attested to by the fact that since the publication of *On Liberty* much of the discussion of the issues of censorship has been conducted on Mill's terms. Despite this, it seems to me that the empiricist assumption which lies at the basis of his attack on censorship is patently false. Strangely, however, when the precise nature of this falsity is established, the case against censorship, far from being weakened becomes unanswerable.

II

Let me begin by indicating certain cases where Mill's thesis *is* false, cases that is where it does not seem possible for my judgments to be fallible. As an indication of one sort of judgment which I have in mind I will mention my certainty that my wife is not an agent of the KGB. I purposely do not express this by saying that my wife is a 'paradigm case' of someone who is not a KGB agent, since whatever the merits of paradigm case arguments in other contexts, I find it difficult to understand what, in this field at least, paradigms are supposed to be. (I would have thought that anyone who *was* a KGB agent would try very hard to avoid any of the features of a paradigm.) Rather what I mean is that the possibility of my wife's working for the Russian Secret Service is not one which I can seriously entertain. True I can *imagine* what future events could lead me to suspect her and to question my judgment. The discovery that my wife had spent her teens in Russia, apparently for no good reason, or that her life with me had been punctuated by the occasional trip to the Russian Embassy in London would obviously cast some doubt on my claim to certainty. Fortunately I am equally certain that I shall discover no such things. I met my wife in her teens, along with numerous friends who had shared her childhood in Wales, and though she has not spent all her life in my company since meeting me, she has certainly not spent enough time apart from me to allow for even occasional day-trips to the Russian Embassy. Again, I am not saying that you, or for the matter the men from MI5, might not entertain doubts on this matter. But this does not affect my certainty. For I am in a much better position to know than either you or MI5. She is, after all, *my* wife.

To say that I am in a better position than others to judge on this issue is not of course to say that I have better reasons for my claim than do others. Once I allow talk of reasons for and against my wife's credibility as a loyal citizen, then it is open to someone of Mill's persuasion to question the worth of my reasons, offer reasons against and in this way to cast doubt on my claim to certainty. But the truth is that I have *no* reasons for my belief. Admittedly it is easy enough to find propositions from which the proposition 'My wife is not a KGB agent' can be derived, for example, 'My wife has had no contact with any official of the Russian Communist Party at any time' or 'My wife would never do anything to further the cause of the USSR', but it is obvious that these are not reasons for my claim, since I am as a matter of fact considerably less certain of their truth than of my original claim. And this is the point. I am as certain of *that* claim as I am of anything in this life. Consequently the idea of using reasons either to support it or to convince me of its falsity is ruled out by the logic of argument. For in any argument we use claims of which someone is more certain to convince them of something of which they are less certain.

What we have here then is, like the example from Wittgenstein mentioned earlier, something whose truth goes without saying. But of course, so far my argument, even if accepted, may seem of doubtful relevance to Mill's points, or to the question of censorship. 'After all', someone may say, 'the interest of Mill's position, at least for your purposes, lies not in its relevance to factual claims, such as your wife's security status, but in its relevance to moral questions. And here the situation is very different, for even if it is admitted that people are sometimes in a position to judge with certainty on factual issues, when we turn to moral issues no one is in any better position to judge than anyone else, and consequently any claims to certainty will be unfounded. The application of moral concepts is, after all, as many contemporary philosophers never tire of pointing out, essentially contested.'

Now there is some truth in this objection to which I shall return later. What is not true is that there is no certainty in the sphere of morality comparable to that which we find with some factual claims. Let me illustrate this by returning to Orwell's criticism of Salvador Dali's autobiography. Orwell's assessment of the book rests largely on various incidents from Dali's life which he relates. These include, from Dali's early childhood, kicking his young sister in the head for fun and throwing a small boy from a suspension bridge for no apparent reason, and in his late teens half-killing a small girl and, this for the feeling of power which it gives him, sexually teasing a young woman who is in love with him for five years and then deserting her. On the basis of these and other similar examples of sadism, Orwell claims that Dali is a 'dirty little scoundrel' and his autobiography 'disgusting', and I might as well say at this point that not only do I agree with Orwell's judgments, but that if anything they seem to err on the side of leniency. I am, that is, certain that Dali's attitude towards the particular people he mentions was despicable. And I say 'the particular people he mentions' not because I have in mind some features which distinguish them from other people, for I have no doubt that the examples he gives are illustrative of Dali's lack of concern for people generally, but simply to rule out the imaginable cases where those kicked, tormented, or otherwise are Hitlers or Ghengis Khans and where my certainty might (*might*) be less. Such cases are imaginable but they do not affect my case here, for I am equally certain that Dali's victims were young children, teenage women and not tyrants or mass-murderers, and that they were abused for fun and not, for example, because of their potential or actual danger to humanity. Indeed, as Orwell points out, it hardly affects the case whether or not the incidents mentioned actually occurred since they are obviously things which Dali would have *liked* to do, and it is the delight in acts of horrific cruelty, imagined or otherwise, which is one of his most repellent features, and which justifies Orwell's assessment of the book as disgusting. Nor am I denying that we can imagine others who might disagree with these judgments. Indeed we scarcely need to imagine this, since we can safely assume that, at least until his alleged conversion to Roman

Catholicism, Dali himself would have disagreed. But, as with my previous case, the possibility of others disagreeing and perhaps being able to offer reasons for so doing, does not affect my own certainty. For again, my certainty that it is despicable to cause suffering to others for the sake of one's own enjoyment, or even, as Dali might claim, for the sake of one's artistic development, is not one which either admits of or requires reasons, since it is among the most fundamental of my moral convictions.

There is, however, an important difference between the two cases, and this brings me back to a point which I indicated earlier. For, when discussing the possibility of my wife's being a KGB agent, I mentioned that my certainty here is a function of my being in a better position to judge than others. The conceptual connection between these notions, that of being in a position to judge and that of certainty, comes out most clearly (though not only) in those cases where we might be inclined to introduce the notion of expertise. If my car will not start, or if I suffer from recurrent headaches, often what I shall do is to consult an expert, an automobile engineer or a doctor. Probably I shall simply leave them with the problem. 'I haven't time to tinker around with the car', I say to the garage mechanic, 'You find out what's wrong.' Or I leave the doctor to carry out some tests and try to forget about the headache. And I shall be certain of their verdicts, primarily to the extent that I suppose them to be in a position to judge. Thus, if my doctor informs me that in his opinion the headache is tension, but that he is referring me to a specialist, my judgment that I am suffering from tension will be more tentative than when the specialist finally confirms the doctor's opinion. For, after all, the specialist, having been through a certain training is therefore in a better position to judge. And there will be many things such as that the earth is approximately round, or that there exists such a city as New York, whose certainty I *never* question, not because I have ever checked myself, but simply because *all* the experts, everyone who is in a position to judge (scientists, astrologers, ship's captains) agrees on them.

Now, it seems clear to me that when we turn to moral issues, the concept of certainty is no longer connected with that of being in a position to judge, or in a position to answer questions or to solve problems, for the simple reason that these notions have no sense here. I have indicated that part of what gives the mechanic or the doctor their expertise is their familiarity with a certain *kind* of problem. And this goes along with certain problems being pretty much the same whoever has them. The motor mechanic can help me with my burnt out clutch because burnt out clutches are similar in important respects, the doctor with my heart attack, because my heart attack and yours are not too dissimilar.

With many moral problems there is nothing like this. In Camus' novel *The Plague* we are presented with the story of various men and women trapped in Oran, a plague-stricken town in Algeria, and central among the book's themes is the different conceptions which people can have of their lives and those they share them with. Some of these are brought to the fore in the relationship of the journalist Rambert and his friend Dr Rieux. Rieux's attitude towards the plague is partly one of resignation. At worst the quarantine laws which prevent his leaving Oran and the enforced isolation from his wife who is in a nearby sanatorium, are necessary evils. At best they are a blessing since they protect her from the plague and provide an opportunity for Rieux to devote himself to relieving the suffering in the town. Either way 'the law was law, plague had broken out, and he could only do what had to be done'.[8]

For Rambert on the other hand, the quarantine laws are simply an obstacle to his reunion with his girlfriend in Paris. Where Rieux sees the restrictions imposed by the plague as facts to be accepted, Rambert sees them as barriers to be overcome. This agreement is brought to a head by Rieux's suggestion that Rambert should join the volunteers engaged in the dangerous task of fighting the plague. Rambert replies:

> Personally I've seen enough of people who die for an idea. I don't believe in heroism; I know its easy and I've learnt that it can be murderous. What interests me is living and dying for what one loves.[9]

Though one might say that in a superficial sense Rieux and Rambert face the same problem, separation from a loved one, this *would* be only in a superficial sense. For the nature of their problems stems from the particular circumstances of their relationships and the particular role which these play in their lives. Rambert sees in the request to join Rieux's campaign, or indeed in the suggestion that he reconcile himself in any way to imprisonment in Oran, a demand that he sacrifice his relationship with his girlfriend for the sake of an empty piece of heroism, for an 'idea'. That is to say, he thinks of his life apart from her, his work as something independent of their relationship, a point brought out earlier in the book when Rieux suggests that the plague at least offers Rambert an unparalleled opportunity to employ his journalistic talents, and Rambert remarks tersely:

> The truth is that I wasn't brought into the world to write newspaper articles. But it's quite likely that I was brought into the world to live with a woman.[10]

Rieux, by contrast, does not see his dedication to medicine as something which stands in the way of his relationship with others, but as a part of what makes him the person he is and hence makes those relationships what they are. But in neither case can the problems faced be separated from the people involved and those they are involved with. And this is generally true of problems connected with personal relationships. That this is one of Camus' main points in the book is shown by his account of how finally preoccupation with the plague and fear of catching it 'killed off the faculty not only of love but even of friendship' in the inhabitants of Oran.

> For the first time exiles from those they loved had no reluctance to talk freely about them using the same words as everybody else, and regarding their deprivation from the same angle as that from which they viewed the latest statistics of the epidemic . . . Obviously all this meant giving up what was most personal in their lives. Whereas in the early days of the plague they had been struck by the host of small details that, while meaning absolutely nothing to others, meant so much to them, personally, . . . now, on the other hand, they took an interest only in what interested everyone else, they had only general ideas and even their tenderest affections now seemed abstract, items of the common stock.[11]

As Camus observes, the uniqueness of a relationship is involved in what makes it one of love or friendship. And it is a corollary of this that where there are problems in such relationships, the problems will themselves be unique. If I have problems in living with my wife and you have problems living with yours, we do not share the same problem. I might have *no* problem living with *your* wife.

True, not all moral problems will be of this sort. And there will be many where we *can* give some sense to the notion of others facing the same problem, so that we may turn to them for advice and help. Sometimes this will be so where, for example, people face problems like unemployment or of conflicts between professional ethics and personal values. But even here no sense can be given to the idea of someone's being in a better position than I to judge. I may ask another's advice, but whether I take it or not is up to me. With a medical problem, I may simply follow the doctor's advice and if things do not turn out as expected, I can disclaim responsibility. ('Don't blame me; the doctor told me just to keep on taking the tablets'.) But it would be simply a bad joke (or the mark of an extreme conventionalist) if, when faced with a serious moral problem, I were to say to someone, 'I'm no good at facing up to these sorts of difficulties, so you tell me what the answer is, and then I shan't need to think about it myself.' As we have seen, with factual issues my certainty often stems from my having taken on trust what those who are in a position to judge have told me. With moral issues, by contrast, my judgment will count as a genuine moral judgment only in so far as it is not taken on trust but one which I have reached for myself. And this is to say that in morality the notion of being in a better position to judge lacks sense.

III

So far the relevance of all this to the issue of censorship may not be obvious. But it becomes clearer when one notices that any form of censorship, in so far as it is justified on moral grounds at all, *can* be justified only on the assumption that some people *are* in a better position to judge than others. Thus, when Orwell suggests that if we share his condemnation of Dali's autobiography we must, even if only imaginatively, be willing to consider the possibility of suppressing the work in question, he is asking us to accept that we should be willing (even if only imaginatively) to countenance a situation in which others allow the judgment that the work is 'debased and disgusting' to be made for them, a situation in which, that is, it makes sense for someone to say, 'I think Dali's work is disgusting because George Orwell says so.' Again, when Tolstoi recommends the suppression of what in his opinion offends against the moral ideals of his age, he not only presupposes a degree of moral consensus which there is no reason to suppose actually obtains, but also implies that his judgment of what is morally offensive is one which others should take on trust. The general point is concisely made by John Anderson.[12] The advocates of censorship, he notes, always 'imply in professing to be able to censor, that they themselves will take no harm from examining what they proceed to suppress; in other words they imply that there is a line of social demarcation between protectors and protected . . .'[13].

What Anderson emphasises in his writings on censorship, and what others who have dealt with the subject both pro and contra have generally ignored, is that the institution of censorship involves not merely a relation between those who censor and those who they censor, but also and more importantly a relation between the censor and those whose access to the censored work is thus impaired. Orwell, for instance, makes considerable play of those features of Dali's work which he finds morally objectionable and, as we have seen, uses these features as grounds for censorship. What he does not discuss is the question whether anyone has the right to prevent others examining these features for themselves and reaching a judgment on them.

Similarly, in recent political discussions about the wisdom or moral propriety of placing limits on free speech, the issue has been expressed almost exclusively in terms of whether or not there are political views so far beyond the pale that no one ought to be allowed to express them, rather than whether there are views which only certain people should be allowed to hear. A few years ago, Professor Roy Edgeley illustrated this perfectly in an article[14] intended to show that the notion of completely free speech is incoherent as an ideal. Edgeley took the specific case of a demonstration at Sussex University in which he was himself involved, and whose object (and result) was to prevent a lecture by the American academic and Vietnam War advisor Thomas Huntingdon, and pointed out that those who opposed the demonstration on the grounds of freedom of speech were themselves, more or less explicitly, proposing various sorts of constraints on this freedom.

> Let's list the various constraints imposed or proposed by different parties in the whole complex of the Huntingdon affair: (1) by some members of Sussex University against Huntingdon, shouting and heckling sufficient to prevent him from speaking on 5 June (2) by some members of Sussex University against Huntingdon, withdrawal of the invitation for 5 June (3) by Huntingdon, against millions of Vietnamese, the direct application of mechanical and conventional power on such a massive scale as to force a massive migration from countryside to city (4) by Crossman[15] against the academics proposing (5) loss of job.[16]

Edgeley goes on to remark that the form of constraint actually imposed by himself was mild compared with the others. What is interesting is that he carefully avoids listing (and indeed at no point in his article mentions) *one* constraint which, mild or severe, might be thought to be at least worthy of notice. What he does not mention is that in preventing Huntingdon from speaking he was also preventing anyone who might have wished (in this case presumably students) from listening.

Though the proponents of censorship whom I have mentioned, Tolstoi, Orwell, Edgeley, differ widely both in the moral standpoints from which they propose censorship, and in the range of objects which they propose to censor, what is common to them is that despite an emphasis on the relationship of their own moral beliefs to the subjects of their moral appraisal (works of art, lectures) none of them discusses the relationship of these moral beliefs

to the moral beliefs of those who will be the victims of their proposed censorship. Nor is this surprising, a mere oversight. On the contrary, it is necessary
to the whole notion of protecting others from corruption which is central to
any defence of censorship that the censor should refuse to judge his own
moral beliefs in the same terms which he applies to those of others. He must,
to use the terms which I have hitherto employed, regard himself as in a
better position to judge. As Anderson indicates, this can be established by a
reductio ad absurdum argument. For let us suppose that it is admitted that the
censor is morally on precisely the same footing as those he claims to protect.
This being so, we can only assume that either he never comes into contact
with any corrupting material, in which case he remains uncorrupted but
without a function, and the institution of censorship is pointless, or he comes
into contact with corrupting material in which case, since he *alone* does so,
he is the member of society most in danger of corruption, and hence least
suited to the post of censor; in which case, the institution of censorship is
dangerous rather than pointless. Thus Edgeley who was evidently
acquainted with Huntingdon's views and uninfluenced by them, since he
claimed to object to them, was seeking to prevent his students from hearing
these views, presumably on the grounds that they *would* be influenced by
them, would be unable to see them for what they were. But a simpler way of
expressing this point would be to say that according to any view of censorship, the censor's view of what is immoral is to be taken on trust by those
whom he claims to protect. Not having been given the opportunity to
consider the alternatives, they are to accept that certain works are obscene,
depraved, evil simply because the censor says so. The censor is given, that is
to say, the role of an expert in a field where expertise, relying as it does on
the notion of 'being in a better position to judge' has been shown to have no
sense.

Now it is at this point that the proponent of censorship can generally be
relied upon to reveal what he regards as his trump card. 'For', he will ask, 'is
it not obvious that whatever arguments may be offered to the contrary, the
notion of being in a position to judge *does* have a part to play, and indeed a
vital part, in morality. For is it not obvious and admitted by all, that whether
Orwell and Tolstoi are in a better position to judge on the moral acceptability
of art than you and I, whether or not Professor Roy Edgeley is in a better
position to judge the acceptability of certain political views than the students
of Sussex University, all of us, Tolstoi, Orwell, Edgeley, University students,
you and I are in a better position to judge on all these issues than (say) a four-
year-old child.' Put briefly, the objection is that censorship is both justified
and indeed essential in the case of children. And since most works of art are
accessible to very young children, is not then censorship necessary to
protect them from corruption?

The answer to this objection is that, far from its being the case that censorship is justified when it has as its aim the protection of young children, it is of
doubtful significance to speak of censorship in this context at all. I have said
that censorship occurs where in one way or another limitations are placed
on those viewpoints which are to be given a hearing. But it seems to me a

precondition of these limitations constituting censorship that the audience under consideration should consist of human beings capable of forming judgments on the basis of what they hear. Or again, I have said that the incoherence of defences of censorship lies in the supposition that sense can be given to the notion that in morality one person may be in a better position to judge than another, but it is a presupposition of this objection that the beings in question are capable of judgment in the first place.

Now where what we have in mind are very small children, it should be obvious that neither of these conditions is satisfied. As we saw at the beginning of this paper, judgment is possible only where certain things are taken for granted, accepted without question. And it follows that if a child is ever to be capable of judging for itself in morality, there will be a stage where it must simply accept certain judgments without question. I may discuss with a ten-year-old child whether stealing is not sometimes justified, for example whether it is not sometimes justified to steal from the rich to give to the poor. But such a discussion can make sense only against a background of the child's having been brought up to accept without question, as say a four-year-old, that stealing is something wrong, something which requires justification. And bringing the child to accept this will no doubt have both its positive and its negative aspects. For it will involve both telling the child that stealing is wrong (and brooking no opposition on this) and keeping the child away from those who would lead it to think otherwise. For a parent or teacher to try to protect young children from those people, those films, those books, which they see as obscene or corrupting cannot intelligibly be condemned (or indeed commended) as an example of censorship, as an interference with the child's freedom of choice, since this would presuppose precisely what is in question, that the child is in a position to choose.

I should, however, emphasise that in saying this I am not repeating one of the points made by Mill in his essay. Mill is emphatic that his opposition to censorship is 'meant only to human beings in the maturity of their faculties', but where I have made the conceptual point that it is coherent to speak of censorship only in respect of a person already capable of reasoned judgment, Mill appears to rest his case on a moral judgment. Censorship, so the argument goes, is an evil. But though still an evil even where young children are involved, in this case it is justified by the child's overriding need for protection. Unfortunately, since it is not only children who we may regard as immature and in need of protection, this argument leads Mill to recommend the most far-reaching censorship.

> It is, perhaps, hardly necessary to say that this doctrine is meant only to apply to human beings in the maturity of their faculties. . . . Those who are still in a state to require being taken care of by others, must be protected against their own actions as well as against external injury. For the same reason we may leave out of consideration those backward states of society in which the race may be considered as in its nonage. . . . Despotism is a legitimate mode of government in dealing with barbarians. . . . [17]

Mill's discussion of these issues is confusing in the highest degree. When I say of a child who is being taught the moral standards which will form the basis of his judgment, that it is immature, I am making a factual judgment about the stage of development which the child has reached, and about which there would be no disagreement except perhaps in borderline cases. By contrast, to say, as Mill does, that certain *adults* in other societies, or perhaps in our own society, are immature,[18] is, if it means anything at all, to make a moral judgment, and one about whose correctness there may be *moral* disagreement. And to say, again as Mill does, that in such cases censorship is permissible, while admittedly a legitimate use of the concept of censorship, involves, like all defences of censorship, the elevation of one set of moral judgments, in this case judgments about maturity, to a privileged position. It is again to adopt the stance of an authority in a context where the notion of an authority has no place. Where the notion does have a sense is in the relationship of parents and teachers to young children. But then, what they do cannot without logical impropriety be termed censorship.

But to say that the relationship of parents and teachers to immature children cannot be characterised as censorship is not to say that this relationship may not itself be the subject of censorship. You cannot subject young children to censorship. What you can do is to subject to censorship the views of parents and teachers *vis-à-vis* their charges' moral education. Thus when the censors of film and television prevent the portrayal of certain subjects or viewpoints on the grounds that they may corrupt the youth, they are guilty of usurpation of the role of parents and teachers in a child's education. And in so far as any defence is offered for this interference the advocate of censorship will once again be committed to the idea that some people are in a better position than others to judge on moral issues—in this case the moral issue of what influence parents should have over their children.

My point here is perfectly illustrated by one of the counsel for the prosecution's opening remarks to the jury in the notorious *Lady Chatterley* trial.

> 'Would you', he asked, 'approve of your young sons, young daughters—because girls can read as well as boys—reading this book. Is it a book that you would have lying around in your own house?'

Mr Griffith-Jones was at this point, of course, trading on the jury's understanding that such questions are ones which it is appropriate for parents to ask, and presumably answer in different ways. What he failed to see was that it was being asked in the course of an argument designed to show that such questions should be asked and answered, not by parents with regard to their own children, but by the twelve just men and true to whom it was addressed. For if the prosecution were successful, then the net result would be to rob parents of choice in this matter.

I said at the beginning of this essay that the institution of censorship does not involve any contradiction, explicit or implicit. But it looks as though the apparent contradiction implicit in Griffith-Jone's argument, can be avoided only on the assumption that the jury were in a better position to judge on this moral question than other parents. But here, as elsewhere, the notion of being in a better position to judge morally is without sense.

NOTES

1   David Hume, *A Treatise of Human Nature* (ed. L A Selby-Bigge) (Oxford, 1965), p. 272.

2   E.g. 'I shall speak of practices where Wittgenstein speaks of language-games.' T Morawetz, *Wittgenstein and Knowledge* (Amherst, 1978), p. 5.

3   L Wittgenstein, *On Certainty* (Oxford, 1974), p. 24.

4   L Tolstoi, *What is Art?*, World Classics Edition (Oxford, 1930), p. 248.

5   *Ibid.* p. 261.

6   George Orwell, 'Benefit of Clergy: Some Notes on Salvador Dali', in *The Collected Essays, Journalism and Letters of George Orwell* (ed. S Orwell and I Angus), vol. III (London, 1968), p. 159.

7   Mill excepts mathematical judgments, but for reasons which do not affect my argument.

8   Albert Camus, *The Plague* (trans. Stuart Gilbert) (Harmondsworth, 1960), p. 73.

9   *Ibid.* pp. 135-6.

10   *Ibid.* p. 72.

11   *Ibid.* pp. 149-51.

12   John Anderson, 'Art and Morality', *Australasian Journal of Philosophy and Psychology*, vol. 19 (1941), p. 279.

13   *Ibid.* p. 280.

14   Roy Edgeley, 'Freedom of Speech and Academic Freedom', *Radical Philosophy*, vol. 10 (1975).

15   R H S Crossman had suggested in a letter to *The Times* that it should be a condition of employment in a University that one neither prevents nor seeks to prevent freedom of speech.

16   'Freedom of Speech and Academic Freedom', p. 11.

17   J S Mill, 'On Liberty', in *Utilitarianism* (ed. Mary Warnock) (Fontana Library, 1970), pp. 135-6.

18   I can attach no sense at all to the suggestion that a race or society as a whole may be immature.

BIBLIOGRAPHY

I have listed books and articles, on theoretical topics, to which references are made in the Introduction and essays and have added a selection of other published work by the contributors on related subjects. I have not listed novels, plays or poems cited in the essays.-PL

ANDERSON, JOHN, 'Art and Morality', *Australasian Journal of Philosophy and Psychology*, vol. 19 (1941)

BEARDSMORE, R W, *Moral Reasoning* (London, 1969)
— *Art and Morality* (London, 1971)
— 'Two Trends in Contemporary Aesthetics', *British Journal of Aesthetics*, vol. 13 (1973)
— 'Learning From a Novel', in *Philosophy and the Arts*, Royal Institute of Philosophy Lectures, vol. 6 (London, 1973)
— 'The Limits of Imagination', *British Journal of Aesthetics*, vol. 20 (1980)

BEARDSLEY, MONROE C, *Aesthetics: Problems in the Philosophy of Criticism* (New York, 1958)
— *The Possibility of Criticism* (Detroit, 1970)
— 'The Concept of Literature', in F Brady, J Palmer and M Price, (eds), *Literary Theory and Structure* (New Haven and London, 1973)

BEARDSLEY, MONROE C and WIMSATT, W K, 'The Intentional Fallacy', *Sewanee Review*, vol. XIV (1946); also in D Newton-de Molina, ed., *On Literary Intention*

BELL, CLIVE, *Art* (London, 1914)

BRADBURY, MALCOLM, *Possibilities: Essays on the State of the Novel* (Oxford, 1973).

BRISSENDEN, R F (ed.), *Studies in the Eighteenth Century* (Canberra, 1968)

BROOKS, CLEANTH, *The Well-Wrought Urn* (New York, 1947).

BURKE, DANIEL, *Notes on Literary Structure* (Washington, 1982)

CLOSE, A J '*Don Quixote* and the 'Intentionalist Fallacy"', *British Journal of Aesthetics*, vol. 12 (1972)

COHEN, TED, 'Why Beauty is a Symbol of Morality', in T Cohen and P Guyer, (eds), *Essays in Kant's Aesthetics* (Chicago, 1982)
— 'Jokes', in Eva Schaper, (ed.), *Pleasure, Preference and Value: Studies in Philosophical Aesthetics* (Cambridge, forthcoming)

CULLER, JONATHAN, *Structuralist Poetics* (London, 1975)
— *The Pursuit of Signs* (London and Henley, 1981)

DANTO, A, *Transfiguration of the Commonplace* (Cambridge Mass., 1981)

DAVIDSON, D, 'Hume's Cognitive Theory of Pride', in *Essays on Actions and Events* (Oxford, 1980)

EATON, MARCIA, 'Art, Artifacts and Intentions', *American Philosophical Quarterly*, vol. 6 (1969)
— 'Good and Correct Interpretations of Literature', *Journal of Aesthetics and Art Criticism*, vol. 29 (1970)

EDGELEY, ROY, 'Freedom of Speech and Academic Freedom', *Radical Philosophy*, vol. 10 (1975)

ELLIS, JOHN, *The Theory of Literary Criticism: A Logical Analysis* (Berkeley and Los Angeles, 1974)

EMPSON, WILLIAM, *Seven Types of Ambiguity* (London, 1953)

ERLICH, VICTOR, *Russian Formalism: History-Doctrine* (The Hague, 1965)

FREGE, GOTTLOB, 'On Sense and Reference', in P Geach and M Black (eds), *Philosophical Writings of Gottlob Frege* (Oxford, 1970).

FRIED, M, *Absorption and Theatricality: Painting and Beholder in the Age of Diderot* (Berkeley, 1980)

FRYE, NORTHROP, *Anatomy of Criticism* (Princeton, 1957)

GALE, R M, 'The Fictive Use of Language', *Philosophy*, vol. 46 (1971)

GARVIN, P L, (ed.), *A Prague School Reader on Aesthetics, Literary Structure and Style* (Washington, 1964)

GEACH, P T, *God and the Soul* (London, 1969)

GOODMAN, NELSON, 'On Likeness of Meaning', *Analysis*, vol. 10 (1949)

HAWKES, T, *Structuralism and Semiotics* (London, 1977)

HOLLAND, NORMAN, *The Dynamics of Literary Response* (New York, 1968)

HOWELL, R, 'Fictional Objects: How They Are and How They Aren't', *Poetics*, vol. 8 (1979)

HUME, DAVID, *A Treatise of Human Nature*, (ed. Selby-Bigge) (Oxford, 1965)

— 'Of Tragedy', in *Essays, Moral, Political and Literary* (Oxford, 1963)

JONES, JOHN, *On Aristotle and Greek Tragedy* (London, 1968)

JUHL, P D, *Interpretation: An Essay in the Philosophy of Literary Criticism* (Princeton, 1980)

KAMES, LORD, *Elements of Criticism* (1762)

KNIGHTS, L C, 'How Many Children Had Lady Macbeth?', in *Explorations* (Harmondsworth, 1946)

LAMARQUE, PETER, 'Truth and Art in Iris Murdoch's *The Black Prince*', *Philosophy and Literature*, vol. 2 (1978)

— Review of S H Olsen, *The Structure of Literary Understanding*, *Philosophical Review*, vol. 88 (1979)

— Review of R Wollheim, *Art and Its Objects*, and N Wolterstroff, *Works and Worlds of Art*, *London Review of Books*, vol. 3, no. 6 (1981)

— 'How Can We Fear and Pity Fictions?', *British Journal of Aesthetics*, vol. 21 (1981)

— 'Bits and Pieces of Fiction', *British Journal of Aesthetics*, forthcoming

LEAVIS, F R, *The Great Tradition* (Harmondsworth, 1962)

— 'Reality and Sincerity', *Scrutiny*, vol. 19

LESKY, ALBIN, *Greek Tragedy*, trans. H A Frankfort (London, 1965)

LODGE, DAVID, *The Modes of Modern Writing* (London, 1977)

LYAS, COLIN, 'The Semantic Definition of Literature', *Journal of Philosophy*, vol. 66 (1969)

— 'Aesthetic and Personal Qualities', *Proceedings of the Aristotelian Society*, vol. LXXII (1971-2)

— 'The Dehumanization of Art', *British Journal of Aesthetics*, vol. 13 (1973)

— 'Personal Qualities and the Intentional Fallacy', in *Philosophy and the Arts*, Royal Institute of Philosophy Lectures, vol. 6 (London, 1973)

MACDONALD, M, 'The Language of Fiction', *Proc. Arist. Soc.*, suppl. vol. XXVII (1954)

MARGOLIS, JOSEPH, *Art and Philosophy* (Brighton, 1980)

MARTIN, R and SCHOTCH, P, 'The Meaning of Fictional Names', *Philosophical Studies*, vol. 26 (1974)

MILL, JOHN STUART, 'On Liberty', in *Utilitarianism*, (ed. Mary Warnock) (Fontana, 1970)

MORAVETZ, T, *Wittgenstein and Knowledge* (Amherst, 1978)

NEWTON-DE MOLINA, D (ed.), *On Literary Intention* (Edinburgh, 1976)

NOWOTTNY, W, *The Language Poets Use* (London, 1962)

NOZICK, R, *Anarchy, State and Utopia* (New York, 1974)

OHMANN, R, 'Speech Acts and the Definition of Literature', *Philosophy and Rhetoric*, vol. 4 (1971)

OLSEN, STEIN HAUGOM 'Authorial Intention', *British Journal of Aesthetics*, vol. 13 (1973)
— 'What is Poetics?', *Philosophical Quarterly*, vol. 26 (1976)
— 'Defining a Literary Work', *Journal of Aesthetics and Art Criticism*, vol. 35 (1976)
— 'Interpretation and Intention', *British Journal of Aesthetics*, vol. 17 (1977)
— 'Do You Like Emma Woodhouse?', *Critical Quarterly*, vol. 19 (1977)
— *The Structure of Literary Understanding* (Cambridge, 1978)
— 'The Concept of Genre', in L Aagaard-Mogensen and G Hermeren (eds), *Contemporary Aesthetics in Scandinavia* (Lund, 1980)
— 'On Unilluminating Criticism', *British Journal of Aesthetics*, vol. 21 (1981)
— 'Literary Aesthetics and Literary Practice', *Mind*, vol. XC (1981)
— 'Text and Meaning', *Inquiry*, vol. 25 (1982)
— 'The 'Meaning' of a Literary Work', *New Literary History*, vol. 15 (1983)

OLSON, ELDER, *Tragedy and the Theory of Drama* (Detroit, 1961)

ORWELL, GEORGE, 'Benefit of Clergy: Some Notes on Salvador Dali', in *The Collected Essays, Journalism and Letters of George Orwell* (London, 1968)

PARSONS, TERENCE, *Nonexistent Objects* (New Haven and London, 1980)

PHILLIPS, D Z, *Through a Darkening Glass* (Oxford, 1982)

PLANTINGA, A, *The Nature of Necessity* (Oxford, 1974)

RICHARDS, I A, *Principles of Literary Criticism* (London, 1924)
— *The Philosophy of Rhetoric* (Oxford, 1936)

SEARLE, JOHN, 'The Logical Status of Fictional Discourse', in *Expression and Meaning* (Cambridge, 1979)

SKINNER, Q, 'Motives, Intentions and Interpretations of Texts', *New Literary History*, vol. 3 (1972)

STURROCK, JOHN, (ed.), *Structuralism and Since* (Oxford, 1979)

TILLYARD, E M W and LEWIS, C S, *The Personal Heresy* (Oxford, 1965)

TODOROV, T, 'Language and Literature', in R Macksey & E Donato, (eds), *The Structuralist Controversy: The Languages of Criticism and the Sciences of Man* (Baltimore, 1972)
— *Littérature et signification* (Paris, 1967)

TOLSTOI, LEO, *What is Art?* (Oxford, 1930)

TORMAY, A, *The Concept of Expression* (Princeton, 1971)

VAN INVAGEN, P, 'Creatures of Fiction', *American Philosophical Quarterly*, vol. 14 (1977)

VICKERS, BRIAN, *Towards Greek Tragedy* (London, 1973)

WALTON, KENDALL, 'How Remote Are Fictional Worlds From the Real World?', *Journal of Aesthetics and Art Criticism*, vol. 37 (1978)

WIDDOWSON, H G, *Stylistics and the Teaching of Literature* (London, 1975)

WILLIAMS, BERNARD, chairman, *Report of the Committee on Obscenity and Film Censorship*, HMSO (London, 1979)

WILSON, EDMUND, *The Shores of Light* (London, 1952)

WIMSATT, W K, 'Genesis: a Fallacy Revisited', in D Newton-de Molina, ed., *On Literary Intention*
— *The Verbal Icon* (Lexington, 1954)

WOLLHEIM, R, *Art and its objects* (New York and London, 1968)

WOLTERSTORFF, N., *Works and Worlds of Art* (Oxford, 1980)

WITTGENSTEIN, LUDWIG, *Philosophical Investigations* (Oxford, 1953)
— *On Certainty* (Oxford, 1974)